RELOCATION
a practical guide

Sue Shortland

Institute of Personnel Management

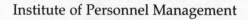

Phototypeset by Wessex Typesetters, Frome, Somerset and printed in Great Britain by LR Printing Services Ltd, Burgess Hill, West Sussex.

British Library Cataloguing in Publication Data
Shortland, Susan M. *1958–*
  Relocation.
  1. Great Britain. Business firms. Relocation
  I. Title
  338.6042
ISBN 0–85292–441–0

The views expressed in this book are the author's own, and may not necessarily reflect those of the IPM.

Contents

List of tables

Acknowledgements

I would like to express my thanks to my colleague Vicky Hibbert for her assistance with the preparation of the text and to Sharon Easton for her excellent typing of the manuscript.

I would also like to thank all the personnel, industrial relations and relocation managers who supplied information and gave up their time to assist in the research and writing of this book and to the staff of the CBI, Industrial Relations Services, the Institute of Manpower Studies and Price Waterhouse, whose reports and publications were a valuable source of information.

Sue Shortland

Introduction

Relocation is a diverse and fast-moving subject. Personnel professionals with responsibility for relocating staff may find themselves having to deal with new recruits who are relocated to take up their appointments, individuals already on the payroll who are required to transfer to another company location, either in their home country or abroad, foreign nationals coming into the UK to work for the company or even a company relocation exercise which involves a transfer of all or part of the organization to a new site – more usually in the UK but possibly abroad, perhaps to Europe.

Relocation creates an impact on pay and benefit packages and on recruitment and training strategies. It also requires some knowledge of taxation and employment law. Relocation involves people: it causes anxiety and stress in the personal lives of all affected. Personnel professionals need to call upon all aspects of their training and personnel experience to manage the relocation process: they must achieve business requirements but at the same time take into account the human needs of those involved. This is no easy task.

Relocation is an emotive subject. It involves transferees moving away from their home locations, away from family and friends, and starting afresh somewhere new. Employees may be required to sell their homes, so personnel responsible for relocation become involved in the vagaries of the housing market. A cost effective relocation package needs to be constructed and used effectively to overcome such problems as house price booms, slumps and large price differentials.

The tax treatment of relocation packages requires careful handling for benefits to be of value to employees but also to be cost effective to companies.

Relocation affects the lives of not just the transferees but also their families. Understanding employees' family concerns and helping to alleviate them goes a long way to reducing employee resistance to relocation. And, with the completion of the Single European Market, more relocation activity is certain to occur within Europe. Personnel professionals must be prepared for this development.

Organizations can gain a greater understanding of how to manage the process by examining the practice of others. This book concentrates on relocation activity within the UK; it draws on the experience of organizations which relocate staff regularly or have undertaken a group move exercise. It examines how to overcome employee resistance, the relocation allowances package, how to tackle moves where large house price differentials are involved, the tax treatment of relocation expenses and group moves. Looking beyond the UK, it also examines the European dimension to relocation and lessons to be learned from the American experience.

1

How to overcome resistance to relocation

Resistance to relocation is growing. Employees refuse to relocate for a number of reasons which include:

- the need to care for dependent relatives
- separation from family and friends
- the fact that the new area appears unattractive
- concern about children's education
- spouse's job/career
- the stress associated with buying, selling and moving
- financial worries.

Employers must take action if they are to overcome the many factors that stand in the way of relocation.

This chapter examines the need for mobility, relocation trends, resistance to relocation and internal and external constraints to mobility. It reviews the barriers to relocation and how to overcome them by providing practical solutions to employees' concerns. It also demonstrates the need to create a mobility culture and how to go about it. Unless stated otherwise, the various sections of this chapter refer to individual employee transfers and group moves.

The need for mobility

Organizations require employee mobility for the purpose of recruitment, internal transfer and company relocation. For employers relocating individual existing staff the reasons behind the need for employee mobility include:

- promotion
- career development
- getting the right person for the right job

1

- to fill a skills gap
- to combat labour shortages
- training and retraining
- imparting skills to others
- remotivation
- an alternative to redundancy
- to improve on poor performance
- as a solution to overstaffing.

Relocation can be required of recruits for three main reasons: finding the right person for the job and to fill skills and labour shortage gaps.

Organizations change their premises for a wide variety of reasons (see Chapter 5). The requirement for employee mobility under such circumstances depends on a number of factors: the need to maintain continuity and production; the ability to attract staff in the new location; and company philosophy towards its employees. For instance, some organizations use a relocation exercise to shake out unwanted personnel and only require mobility from key employees. Others look to relocate certain departments with specialized knowledge and skills, recruiting such personnel as clerical and support staff in the new location. Some firms are guided by company philosophy and expect mobility from all employees, as all personnel from the managing director to the shop floor workers are regarded as equally important to the future of the business.

Managerial responsibility for relocation should rest with named individuals. This is usually the case when a company is undertaking a group move and senior management sees the need to focus clearly on the relocation process.

The pattern of demand for individual relocations can vary widely within and between organizations depending on their structure and the state of the labour market. So frequently responsibility for handling individual transfers does not lie within one person's remit, instead, moves are organized by different managers according to the needs of different departments.

Relocation is, in effect, the product of supply and demand: the employer's demand for mobility and the employees' readiness to accept it. As a result it is important to understand why and when relocation is necessary, how to predict mobility and how to encourage it.

Relocation trends

Numbers moving

According to statistics published in 1986 by the CBI Employee Relocation Council, around 250,000 people move home each year for work-related reasons. This figure includes individuals being relocated by their companies, recruits moving to take up employment and organizations moving their workforces to new sites. The figure does not include employees changing homes on retirement. This figure may have risen slightly more recently but it probably still represents the scale of relocation today.

Research conducted by the Institute of Manpower Studies[1] in 1987 into the mobility of managerial and professional staff indicated that corporate demand for mobility was not rising sharply. However, more recent research on individual employee moves conducted by Industrial Relations Services,[2] shows that the overall number of job moves taking place is increasing. Of the 67 organizations interviewed in early 1989, nearly two thirds said that they were either relocating similar numbers as in the past or had increased the number of relocations (21 and 40.4 per cent respectively).

Direction

There is little evidence on the directions in which transfers take place. Because of the high cost and inherent problems of relocating employees backwards and forwards across the North-South divide, companies increasingly attempt to regionalize career moves so that employees can gain promotion and/or experience within, or as close as possible to, their home locations. However, around 40 per cent of the relocations reported in the Institute of Manpower Studies[1] research were across the North–South divide, with the south receiving five northerners for every three southerners going north.

Types and structure of mobility

Traditionally, managerial and professional staff relocate for developmental purposes – with promotion and career enhancement being the main reasons for moving. Relocation is a costly exercise. Companies, therefore, give careful consideration before any moves are made. Relocation for its own sake is rare.

However, the structure of mobility is changing. In 1987, the Institute of Manpower Studies[1] observed that relocation was being used increasingly to counter labour shortages in particular occupations (shortage skills) and that more pressure was brought to bear on employees in specialist occupations to relocate to fill skills gaps (specialist skills). Also there was greater demand for those on accelerated development programmes (high fliers) to relocate.

In 1989, this finding was confirmed by the Industrial Relations Services research.[2] In the main, it found that the mix of employees relocating had stayed roughly the same, with the traditional groups of managerial and professional staff being affected. However, 18 per cent of the survey sample reported that different categories of staff are now being asked to move – those who have traditionally not been regarded as being so mobile. These include specialist computer staff (specialist skills), management trainees (usually the high fliers) and clerical staff (shortage skills).

However, a clear distinction arose in Industrial Relations Services research between the reasons for relocating existing staff and new recruits. Despite growing skills and labour shortages, companies are unlikely to move existing employees to ease these problems. Existing staff are more likely to be relocated for developmental reasons. Recruitment is generally seen as the best way to tackle such shortages, with relocation assistance forming a key element in the recruitment strategy. However, Industrial Relations Services found that skills and labour shortages were given less priority by employers than other more strategic considerations – the most important being the need to have the right person for the right job.

Industrial Relations Services also examined relocation by industry group. Although it discovered little variation in the reasons for relocation, it did find that certain industries had a greater tendency to use relocation as an alternative to redundancy. These included: engineering; food, drink and tobacco; general services; general manufacturing; and public services. These industries were also the least likely to relocate people as a means of combating skills shortages, with only general manufacturing tending to employ relocation for this purpose.

Resistance to relocation
Anecdotal evidence suggests that resistance to relocation by employees is increasing. Survey evidence of employers and employees does not provide a clear cut answer, although it does, usually back up the anecdotal view.

In the Institute of Manpower Studies 1987 research, the managers interviewed believed that employees were becoming less willing to relocate. Of the employees themselves, about one-third of the 1,851 surveyed had decided against a relocation within the previous 10 years; half of these had not applied for advertised vacancies and the remainder either applied and then turned down the offer or had refused an employer-requested move.

Research carried out at around the same time by the relocation management company Merrill Lynch[3] indicated that one in seven workplaces (14 per cent) found that the level of resistance to relocation had increased. The survey was based on interviews with 305 major British organizations which relocated staff (excluding central and local government) employing over 250 employees. The survey also found that those firms which moved more than 50 employees each year were more likely to find growing employee resistance than those which moved relatively few employees (nine or fewer).

In the Industrial Relations Services survey on relocation carried out in 1989, of the 59 organizations providing information on employee resistance, 59 per cent said that they had not detected any hardening of employees' attitudes to relocation. However, the remaining 41 per cent said that employee resistance to relocation was increasing.

A different response, however, comes from the employees themselves. During the last week of October 1988, *The Guardian* newspaper published a survey entitled 'Why Work' as a follow up to its previous 'People at Work' surveys carried out in 1970 and 1981. As reported in *Personnel Management*,[4] the Why Work survey attracted 25,973 responses, mainly from 25 to 44 year old managers, professionals and executives. It pointed to a highly mobile workforce which changed jobs frequently and indicated a willingness to relocate within and outside the UK. The survey found that 37 per cent of respondents had moved home for their present job and 56 per cent would consider moving home for their next job.

However, it is likely that although more than half the respondents would consider moving home for their next job, they might not actually do so if they had the option of an equally attractive but more local job. There may also be a difference in attitude between employees beginning a new or enhanced career with a different employer and those asked to accept an internal transfer.

Resistance to relocation is costly. The relocation management company PHH Homequity carried out a survey of job mobility[5] in 1987 and found that seven out of 10 British companies believe that resistance to relocation costs them between £3,000 and £4,000 every time an employee refuses to relocate. These costs are incurred through executive time searching for a replacement, recruitment and advertising; not having the right person in the job at the right time and administration.

Predicting mobility

Predicting employees' willingness to relocate can be a hit or miss affair, especially in the case of a group move. Employers can reduce the likelihood of refusal by making use of self-selection techniques, such as advertising vacancies internally so that only those willing to relocate apply. However, this may not mean that the employer's first choice receives the new job and transfer. Without the benefit of the results of an employee attitude survey, employers planning group moves often have little idea of the percentage take up of relocation – and even attitude surveys may not present a true picture if employees say, on paper, that they will move while in reality they are still weighing up the pros and cons.

To predict mobility employers usually turn to their personnel records to gain some information about employees' personal circumstances. In its research into the mobility of individual managers and professional staff, the Institute of Manpower Studies found that willingness to relocate is strongly related to age, with the younger workforce (those aged between 25 and 35) being the most mobile, with willingness to move declining with age. The 50–55 year olds, however, show greater mobility than the 45 to 50 and the 55 to 60 age bands.

Men are more likely to move than women, although female professional staff are by no means immobile. Employment of the spouse correlates with a lower degree of mobility, as does having children under 18 living at home.

Dependent relatives are an important factor. The research found that over 75 per cent of those with dependent relatives had not moved during the previous 10 years. Qualifications are also important – graduates are more likely to move than non-graduates. The survey also found that those with experience of relocation early in their careers are more likely to relocate again than those who have less or no experience of relocation.

Of those refusing relocation, those in the age group 35–50 are less likely to relocate; they are more likely to be married, have children at home or dependants at home or living nearby.

Internal and external constraints
The decision to accept a relocation is based on the relative importance to the employee and family of various internal (company) and external factors. In the Institute of Manpower Studies research into individual employee mobility, seven internal factors were mentioned by managers and professional staff who agreed to relocate. In order of importance these were:

- improvement to career prospects
- provision of new work experience
- good relocation assistance provided by employer
- higher salary in the new job
- improvement of job security
- establishing new work relationships
- the availability of training/retraining in the new job.

These factors are also important to all types of employees when they change jobs as *The Guardian*'s 1989 'Why Work' survey indicated.[4] It found that the top five main reasons for changing jobs were:

- wanting more experience
- lack of opportunity for promotion
- wanting a change
- good job offered
- wanting more money.

A particularly interesting finding was that twice as many respondents wanted more experience than wanted more money (18 and 9 per cent respectively). Organizations, therefore, need to ensure that their staff are able to achieve greater experience within their work place, before they leave to find it with another employer. This may mean relocation for experience sake.

Just under 2,000 employees who decided not to relocate were interviewed as part of the Institute of Manpower Studies research. The following factors, in order of importance, were identified as being either very important or fairly important in their decision not to accept relocation: moving away from relatives or friends;

spouse/partner/children did not like proposed move; destination was a less attractive area; inadequate salary increase; effect of move on dependent relatives; disruption to children's schooling; difficulties in buying/selling homes; inadequate financial assistance from employer; time and effort involved in moving home; spouse/partner would have difficulty finding job in new area; harmful effect on career of spouse; and move would not have advanced career. Many of these are factors external to the company but employees are likely to attach varying levels of importance to them depending on their own personal circumstances. All these factors are dealt with in this chapter.

Predicting general levels of mobility is all very well but employers need the right people in specific jobs at a certain time. This applies to both individual employee moves and company relocation exercises. The cost of a refusal to move can be high. To encourage mobility, employers need to create a mobility culture by ensuring that the internal factors work in favour of change and to reduce resistance to relocation by minimizing the external problems that discourage employees from moving.

Encouraging mobility – problems and solutions

Problem: moving away from relatives or friends
Surveys from Merrill Lynch and the Institute of Manpower Studies both show that having to move away from relations and/or friends is one of the main reasons given by employees who refuse to move. It is also one of the hardest factors for employers to tackle through policy and practice. Good career and job prospects inside work may not compensate for an active social life outside work.

Nevertheless, there are some steps that employers can take even on this highly personal issue to reduce resistance. These include providing written details of churches, clubs, societies and other activities in the new area which might appeal to the employee, spouse or children. If the company already has a workforce in the new location, it can ensure that employees moving there and their families meet other staff members so that they have the chance to make friends and find out about local events. Employees can also be told about the facilities available in the company's sports and social club.

Financial compensation for the loss of club fees and unexpired subscriptions are often given as part of the disturbance allowance.

In a CBI Employee Relocation Council survey of relocation allowances policies,[6] only one company stated that it paid for employees to join a club in the new area by giving payments in addition to the disturbance allowance. For working parents with children the loss of child care facilities may discourage them from relocating. Assistance with finding new child care arrangements may help solve this problem.

Although these measures are all relatively inexpensive, they show that the company recognizes that employees and their families do face problems in building a new social life and go some way towards helping them to overcome them.

Some relationships may be broken by the proposed move which will cause problems to the family in the future. Medical evidence has shown that wives of relocated employees, in particular, often suffer stress and anxiety as a result of being separated from their parents by long-distance moves. This is especially the case if the woman is not working but is at home bringing up young children and relying on her parents for advice and support.

Such potential problems may prevent the relocation from taking place at all or, if it goes ahead, stress may result in a strain on the marriage and, indirectly, on the employee's performance at work. Employer-sponsored counselling may assist in identifying and alleviating such problems. Although such counselling may be carried out by trained personnel staff, many employees and spouses may not wish to reveal their problems to their employers, fearing that it may jeopardize chances of promotion. A third party counselling organization, paid for by the company, may provide the answer.

Problem: spouse/partner/children do not like the proposed move
Companies generally spend considerable time and effort in talking to employees about a proposed move. Employees have their chance to ask questions, raise problems and find out directly the advantages and disadvantages. As a result they may be keen to relocate, half-hearted about the issue or completely devastated.

Employers should remember that regardless of the impression they have made on the employees, they, in turn, have to relay the news to the, perhaps unsuspecting, family at home. Questions will immediately arise and if the employee cannot answer them, the spouse and children are likely to react negatively.

As a first step, communication with employees is crucial. If they are keen to relocate, they may be able to convince their families.

If they are half-hearted or completely shell-shocked by the idea, the chance of the family liking the prospect is slim.

However, the spouse and family want to know what it means personally for them. The key lies in involving them too. Companies need to provide relevant information for them and answer questions. Employers are increasingly realizing that the final decision as to whether or not to move is often made by the spouse. As a result spouses are generally invited into the company to learn about the move and can travel with the employees to view the new area, househunt, etc.

The children are important too. They may be afraid of leaving friends, going to new schools and living in a strange area. Although full family involvement in relocation planning is not very common in the UK, in America – where relocation techniques are more advanced than in the UK – assistance and information for children is increasingly seen as fundamental to a successful relocation. For employers in the UK to reduce family resistance to relocation, the needs and interests of the family must be considered.

Practical help for all the family includes involvement, discussions, meetings, tours and trips, information provision and having a co-ordinator in-company who is available to talk to spouses and the children if necessary, to help resolve problems.

Communications materials used to promote the concepts of relocation should be of interest to everyone at home, not just the employee. Again, the fact that people can see that the company cares goes a long way to reducing resistance to relocation and can be achieved through thoughtful policies and practice at low cost.

Problem: destination is less attractive
Employees and their families may be unwilling to move because they believe that the new area offers a lower quality of life, or is perceived as unpleasant in some way. Employees may base their decision on preconceived ideas, myths and hearsay without actually seeing the new location.

According to the research carried out by the Institute of Manpower Studies, perceptions of different regions in the UK can present a barrier to relocation. *The Guardian*'s 'Why Work' survey[4] also drew this conclusion. It found that Northern Ireland and London were the least favoured locations (52 per cent and 24 per cent respectively of the survey sample would least like to work there). The South East (excluding London) came third with 9 per cent not wanting to work in the region. (All other regions scored between 3 and 7 per cent.) The most popular area in which to work was Wales and the South West (17 per cent).

Although it is difficult to define 'quality of life', this factor is one of the most important to employees and their families. The University of Glasgow[7] in its research into the quality of life in British cities examined a number of factors including levels of crime and social services (such as health services, education, recreation and sports facilities), the cost of living and cost of housing, labour market opportunities and physical environment. Pollution and shopping facilities are also considered to be important.

Britons would ideally choose to live in a place that has low crime rates, good health facilities, low levels of pollution, a low cost of living, good shopping facilities and good race relations. In its first study of British cities and its second research effort into intermediate cities and towns,[8] the University of Glasgow found that Edinburgh and Plymouth are the top two British cities and Exeter, Halifax, Dundee and York lead the rankings for quality of life offered in intermediate cities.

Although employers may not be aware of each individual's concerns and priorities they can take action to dispel myths and present an accurate and balanced picture of the new area. The solution lies in communication: good, balanced communication is important both for the relocation of individuals and for groups.

Employers usually put more effort into their communications campaigns for group moves than they do for individual transfers. Suggestions for methods of communicating information about an area include:

- an information room inside the company with maps, photographs, house price information
- an information kit or pack for employees to keep with user-friendly local information
- videos on the new area for employees to take home
- slide shows for employees and their families
- informal and/or formal presentations and question and answer sessions
- coach trips to the new area and guided tours
- discussions with local employees who know the area
- newsletters with area information and other details on the move.

Printed information on local areas is relatively inexpensive and gives the employee and family useful facts and figures. However, it is no substitute for seeing the area. A visit to the new location can either confirm the employee's worst fears or, more usually, turn doubt into pleasant surprise.

Videos are expensive to produce. Employees and their families are used to high quality television so an amateurish video is likely to do more harm than good. If the cost is prohibitive, a slide show is a cheaper alternative.

When individuals are asked to relocate, employers do not generally invest in expensive media such as videos, assuming the relocations are 'one-offs'. However, it may be worthwhile to find out how many staff are asked individually to move to particular company locations. The numbers may be surprisingly high and may justify spending money on slides and videos. Employers should remember that facilities in locations do change and that any information provided may have a relatively short shelf-life.

Other methods of communication can easily be used for individual transfers. Information packs are essential as is arranging for viewing trips. Individuals and their families can learn a great deal by meeting existing staff and their families in the new location.

Problem: high cost of housing in destination area
It is not surprising that employees refuse to relocate if they cannot afford to live in the new area. This problem is compounded by the fact that dual income families may lose one income for a period while the spouse finds work – perhaps with no guarantee of equivalent salary.

Housing costs are a major problem for employers as well as for employees. As a result, relocation allowances policies generally provide some form of additional housing cost support, either in the form of an additional housing cost allowance or a low-interest loan. Details are given in the next chapter. To help bridge the so-called North–South divide, employers are adopting a number of more imaginative solutions, including equity sharing, assistance with equity financing, company housing, two homes allowances and shared ownership schemes. However, industrial relations difficulties may result from employees working side by side if some are receiving several thousand pounds worth of mortgage support or subsidized housing while local staff receive no benefits towards their house purchase. Details of the advantages and pitfalls of these are given in Chapter 3, with the tax implications of the various allowances and housing arrangements given in Chapter 4.

Help with high housing costs is an expensive item in the relocation allowances policy. Employers may wish to reconsider relocation of individuals or of the company itself if it means moving into an expensive area. For individual transfers, the same objectives may be achieved (e.g. promotion, career development) through a more local move or a regional move rather than relocation to and from high cost areas.

Problem: inadequate salary increase
Employees may not view relocation as being worth all the disruption and upheaval if their pay packets at the end of the day do not provide compensation. This is a major problem for employers working within fairly rigid salary structures. However, employers can alleviate this by emphasizing the value of the move to the individual's long term career development. The financial benefits available under the relocation policy should be spelled out. If the relocation involves the loss of an area allowance, such as London weighting, such payments may be phased out gradually rather than withdrawn immediately the move takes place (see Chapter 2).

Problem: effect of move on dependent relations
Dependent relatives are very likely to prevent employees from relocating and employers usually have to accept this. Elderly and/or disabled relatives may tie an employee and family down to the area where care can be provided. Employers, however, can do a little to help here. Depending on the employee's and family's circumstances and how care is provided, it may be possible for the employee to relocate to the new job and leave the family in the old location, especially if it is envisaged that the posting is likely to be short term. Employers should think carefully before proposing this option, as splitting a family with heavy responsibilities may result in stress, anxiety, even divorce. Another option is for the employer to provide information on available care in the new location. It may be that the family is unaware of facilities in the new area: health provision varies throughout the country. The University of Glasgow's research into quality of life provides an insight into areas with excellent health care. Further information on health and welfare could be provided by the company at little cost: this could include hospitals and day care facilities as well as special schools for disabled children.

Problem: disruption to children's schooling

Parents with children at critical stages in their education are unlikely to be willing to move home if it means interrupting the child's courses of study and examinations. Quality of education may vary from one location to another and different schools offer different subjects. Moving schools may entail children having to drop preferred subjects or follow different curricula, set texts, etc. The introduction of the core curriculum should help ease this problem but employees with school age children will still be reluctant to move children before and during examination times.

Even if parents are prepared to move, problems arise in trying to identify suitable schools, find out about curricula and facilities. Home search in a new location must inevitably follow after school search, as parents do not wish their offspring to undertake long journeys to and from school.

It is, therefore, not surprising that research conducted recently by the University of Sheffield[9] indicated that 44 per cent of relocating families with school children reported disruption to children's education as being stressful or very stressful. A further 42 per cent said that their children losing friends as a result of the move proved to be a significant source of stress.

Research has also shown that the behaviour of children affects their parents' attitudes to work. If children become disruptive or their attainment records fall, parents believe they are failing their children and begin to question their abilities as parents and the effect that their jobs are having on their home and family life. Employees' work performance may well suffer as a result.

Action to reduce these problems falls into three main categories: financial; timing flexibility and ensuring educational continuity; education counselling and school search assistance.

It is employers' traditional response to attempt to solve the problem through financial support. Although welcomed by parents, this does not address many crucial issues and is not enough in itself. Financial help traditionally includes compensation towards new school uniforms and may cover books and tuition fees as appropriate. Some companies provide compensation for loss of school fees if the child is moved before the end of the academic year or term, or the payment of school fees so that the child may remain at school for the remainder of the academic year/term or until critical examinations are taken. Details of compensation are given in the next chapter.

Flexibility on the timing of the assignment to ensure educational continuity is also becoming common. Delaying the employee and family's relocation for a few weeks or months may mean the difference between acceptance or rejection of a move. However, operational requirements and company needs have to be balanced with employee demands and often a compromise is necessary. For example, temporary accommodation policies may be used to enable the employee to relocate before the family, so that the children's requirements and the company's operational needs are met.

If the need for educational continuity exceeds the typical three month period of the temporary accommodation allowance, help may be given with the upkeep of two homes – one in the new area, the other in the old – until the whole family can move to the new location. An alternative is for the family to move to the new location while the organization pays for boarding school costs or board and lodging for the child until the course of study is completed. Details of this type of financial help are also given in the next chapter.

If it is possible for the child to relocate with the family to the new area, suitable schools need to be found. In a typical relocation exercise employees and their spouses usually have about three months to find houses, schools and move. Employees involved in a group move may have considerably longer: as much as two years. Nevertheless, although time puts pressure on individuals involved in relocation, both individuals and those in groups face similar problems: namely how to identify suitable schools. Parents may find it difficult to judge what makes a good school. Faced with a bewildering variety of prospectuses (of varying quality), they need to identify likely schools, visit them and enrol their children. Bearing in mind that in many families both parents are working, the time to do this properly is rarely available. Employers can help by granting time off for school and home search, by providing information packs with contact names and addresses for schools (of all types: grammar, comprehensive, state and public) and by giving allowances towards the cost of travel to and from the new location. Home search agents usually have a good knowledge of schools in their area and can provide help on identifying suitable schools and housing.

Even with this assistance school search is not easy and parents and children may require educational counselling to identify children's requirements and how these might best be met. Information and advice on schools catering for children with special needs may also be required.

Personnel departments rarely have this knowledge and expertise in-house so a third party education consultant may be needed (see Appendix 2).

Problem: difficulties in buying/selling homes
The whole process of buying and selling property is daunting to most people. Housing is, after all, the most expensive investment most people ever make.

Finding a suitable property in a new location many miles away is a difficult task, especially when both partners are working. Employers usually help by granting paid time off for househunting and travel and meal allowances (see next chapter for details).

Further assistance may be given by engaging the services of a relocation agent to seek property on the family's behalf. These home search agents operate by interviewing the family to determine requirements, collecting and screening housing details in the new area and then drawing up a viewing schedule for the family. This is advantageous because employees do not waste valuable time visiting unsuitable properties and, with a well-arranged viewing schedule, they do not have to cover the same ground twice or have long periods of wasted time. The use of a home search agent can reduce the need for paid time off for househunting, although the cost to the employer of engaging such a service may be considered high at around £1,000 per property or 1 per cent of the purchase price.

Selling property can prove to be an even greater nightmare for employees. They are expected to start work in the new location on a particular date yet, if the housing market is slow or if potential buyers drop out of the housing chain, they may find they have not been able to sell their old home on time or that no new house is available in the new location. They face the uncertainty of living in temporary accommodation, being separated from families and perhaps incurring bridging loan interest.

Employers generally help with the financial burden by paying temporary accommodation costs, travel home at weekends and interest on bridging loans. But such payments are usually subject to a time limit. As a result, to assist in property sale and purchase, an increasing number of employers operate guaranteed home sale schemes, either themselves or through a third party relocation management company. In-house operated guaranteed sale price schemes involve tying up company finance in housing directly or funding a bridging loan.

About 15 per cent of companies which offer bridging finance in some form use a third party relocation management company's guaranteed home sale scheme. This undoubtedly reduces the burden of buying and selling for employees and is, therefore, seen as a valuable employee benefit. A third party may also reduce employers' costs and also the time spent by personnel staff in handling relocation concerns (see Appendix 2).

Under a typical guaranteed home sale scheme, the third party relocation company 'buys' the employee's home for an agreed guaranteed price based on the average of two or three independent valuations. (Title does not change hands, however, and so no stamp duty is payable at this stage; stamp duty is only payable by the final buyer when the house is sold on.) The relocation company in effect, acts as a 'cash buyer' and provides the funds, up to the level of the guaranteed price, to the employee. The employee is then at the end of the housing chain in the new location and so should be able to buy property there more quickly. It is then up to the relocation company to sell the old home on to the eventual buyer.

Some relocation companies are linked to estate agency chains, others are independent. However, because of their experience of the property market, they have the ability to sell more quickly and efficiently than employees can. Because they can give estate agents bulk business they can put pressure on estate agents to sell houses fast. They also use reputable surveyors and valuers to ensure as accurate a valuation as possible, so that the house is put on the market at a price that should ensure a speedy sale.

For this service, employers pay a management fee to the third party (negotiable but in the region of £1,250 to £1,500 per property). On top of this, employers pay fees incurred by the relocation company, for instance estate agents' fees, legal fees, interest on the loan given to the employee and any other costs incurred by the relocation company in the process of acquiring and selling the house. Some savings may be made compared with traditional bridging: if the sale is speedy, the period of bridging is reduced.

Sometimes it may be necessary to sell the house at a price below the guaranteed price already given to the employee. In these circumstances, employers make up the shortfall. (It may be less expensive to drop the asking price of the property rather than continue to fund bridging.) Usually, the house is put on the market for a short while at a price above the guaranteed price. If it sells

for more than the guaranteed price it is up to the employer to
decide what happens to the excess. Usually it is given to the
employee but employers may keep any profit themselves or split
it with the employees: this depends on company policy. Further
details of the allowances given by companies under guaranteed
home sale schemes are given in the next chapter. The tax
implications of guaranteed home sale schemes are given in
Chapter 4.

Employees' resistance to relocation may be reduced by the offer
of benefits such as third party help or traditional bridging finance.
However, other issues in the buying and selling process can also
discourage mobility. Advice may be required on mortgages,
insurance, etc.

Problem: inadequate financial assistance from employer
The Institute of Manpower Studies research found that 'a significant
minority of employees simply did not know what help they could
expect from their employer on relocating. Documentation from
employers tended to be weighty, impenetrable and not widely
available'. Industrial Relations Services also found that guidelines
on eligibility for relocation allowances were unclear, with many
elements of the policy left to the discretion of management.
Policies generally are not user-friendly and not designed to be
of service to the mover. Instead, they are designed for the
administrative convenience of the personnel department. They are
rarely flexible in approach to meeting employees' needs and
employees view the prospect of claiming relocation expenses and
dealing with administration as being too complicated. The Institute
of Manpower Studies research also found that 'the most sought-
after items of financial help were larger disturbance allowances
and high cost area compensation'.

There are a number of steps that employers can take to improve
their relocation allowances policies and the financial assistance
provided, without raising costs.

Clearly written, concise, relocation guidelines could be produced
for employees, which state the allowances available and the method
by which they are paid. These guidelines should state whether
employees are required to keep and/or submit receipts. Although
it raises costs, companies could produce videos to explain the
financial package so that employees could show this to their
families.

Employees need to know what relocation means to them. They

must, therefore, know where they stand on eligibility. A covering letter to each individual could state their eligibility to each item in the policy. Employees should not have to wade through complex paragraphs to find out their entitlements.

Employees' requirements for assistance are likely to vary: some may need financial assistance to buy new school uniforms, others who have no children, may have other requirements. A flexible relocation policy could enable employees to spend money on the items they consider to be most important. Some relocation policies already operate along these lines by providing a sum of money to be spent as the employee and family see fit on such items as househunting and temporary accommodation, but full 'cafeteria style' policies are rare. However, to help reduce resistance to relocation in the United States, flexible policies are beginning to be introduced, despite the fact that this can increase administration time. To reduce the administrative burden on both personnel and relocated employees, employers should examine their current procedures and simplify them where possible.

It is not surprising that employees require additional finance to move into high cost areas or to compensate them for disturbance and the indirect costs of moving. Although employers would not wish to throw money at the problem, they can improve payments to employees by ensuring tax efficiency. Also by reclaiming VAT where possible, companies can reduce costs and, perhaps, plough this money back into increased allowances for employees. Chapter 4 explains how money can be saved through tax efficient relocation policies and through VAT recovery.

Problem: time and effort involved in moving home
Moving home causes major disruption. Visits need to be made to the new area to find suitable accommodation and family time must be spent packing, making arrangements, moving, and unpacking and settling in. Sometimes the prospect of all this upheaval is enough to discourage mobility but steps can be taken by employers on this aspect of moving too. Employees may be granted paid time off for househunting and moving home with provision made for meals, transport and accommodation costs for the employee and spouse, even for the family. Alternatively, childminders' expenses may be paid while the couple househunt (see Chapter 2). Time off is increasingly featured in relocation policies as they are updated and new benefits introduced.

To help employees in the househunting process, it is useful if employers supply details of the new location including access to schools and amenities as detailed above. There are many home search/relocation agencies operating within the UK, each specializing in finding property and schools, in their local area. The cost of engaging such an agency (often set at 1 per cent of the purchase price or around £1,000 per transaction) can reduce the househunting burden on employees and cut down on requirements for time off and cash help. Home search agencies can also manage the transfer of utilities and the removals process.

Reputable removal companies offer a greater level of service than just transporting goods to the new location. Specialist packing and unpacking services are available. Making all the arrangements necessary, such as organizing disconnection and reconnection of utilities, telephone, etc. is an unwelcome chore. Employees who benefit from the services of a third party relocation company have the burden of moving significantly reduced. Help is given with virtually all aspects of buying and selling and arrangement of services and removals is also possible. However, the costs to employers may be considered high.

Checklists for moving are very useful. Removal companies, some relocation companies and the CBI Employee Relocation Council provide these free of charge.

Problem: spouse/partner would have difficulty finding work in the new area

More and more families rely on both partners working. Relocated employees are, therefore, likely to have a working spouse and relocation may result in loss of the second income for a period.

The financial aspects of this particular barrier to relocation are beginning to be tackled by employers, although direct financial help is rare. Compensation for the spouse's income is paid by a few companies but is usually limited to a couple of months' pay less any unemployment benefit received by the spouse. Details of such company policies are given in the next chapter.

Money may provide some compensation for job and income loss and help reduce the family's anxieties about meeting their financial commitments but it may not resolve the spouse's immediate problem of job hunting in a new, strange area. Employers can take steps to ease these problems, for example, by assisting spouses with the preparation of CVs, allowing the use of internal facilities such as photocopying and having personnel staff available to advise and counsel spouses on preparation for a new job. Help in the new area may be given through contacts with other local employers, local chambers of commerce and the use of, and the introduction to, recruitment agencies. Area information guides may provide details of local employers so that spouses can write to them direct. Although some companies have a policy not to employ husband and wife, others may offer jobs to relocated spouses where appropriate.

In 1986, the CBI Employee Relocation Council conducted a survey[10] of its members to examine assistance given to spouses. Out of 45 replies about half provided counselling for employees and spouses, with the majority using internal personnel staff rather than external consultants. However, counselling was, in the main, limited to the relocation allowances package and the new job. A few companies did provide counselling to assist with areas of difficulty raised by the employee and spouse. Only 13 organizations, however, gave assistance with job search: this ranged from contacting local employers and using recruitment agencies to employing spouses within the company. Flexibility on the timing of relocation was also considered, if this helped the spouse in finding a job.

However, some employers did not see that the provision of job search assistance for spouses lay within their area of responsibility. One company noted that it 'takes the view that it can assist and/or compensate for the direct effects of relocation on the employee, but not for the consequential effect on his spouse or other members of his family'.

Employers were more helpful, however, if both the employee and spouse were employed by the company. In such cases job search help may be given or even simultaneous relocation considered.

In 1989, the Council carried out a follow up survey[11] of its members. This indicated that spouse issues were becoming increasingly important to employers. Of 130 responses however, only 9 per cent had a formal policy on spouse assistance. Of these 30 per cent gave financial compensation whilst 70 per cent gave career counselling, CV preparation help and job search assistance.

In line with the Council's earlier survey, many companies (41 per cent) help in an informal way. The assistance given includes financial compensation (4 per cent), career counselling (33 per cent), CV preparation (33 per cent), job search assistance (55 per cent), employment in company (41 per cent). The survey also found that half the companies would not distinguish between

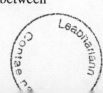

spouses and non-married partners – assistance would be available to both.

Problem: harmful effect on spouse's career
Although linked with the problem of the spouse's job loss, this barrier to relocation can prove almost impossible to remove. If spouses have a successful career, maybe even their own business, it may not be possible to continue this in the new location. Employers can assist spouses in such circumstances with advice on job opportunities for their chosen profession in the new location but such advice and any financial compensation offered is unlikely to provide a solution.

Employers may need to consider other options if they are convinced that they need the chosen employee in the new location. One alternative is that of splitting the couple by the provision of allowances to maintain two homes with travel home at weekends – although by doing this, employers may, in effect, be subsidizing divorce. A second option may lie in career counselling for the spouse. A specialist counsellor can assist in suggesting the most appropriate career choices, with emphasis on career planning and skills analysis. Through such help, spouses may decide to further their careers in a different way or embark on other careers in the new location, with the goal of improving their skills, abilities and marketability for the future.

If career counselling does not provide an answer for the spouse, the couple are faced with a difficult decision – accept relocation and lose one person's career, or not move at all. Couples may need guidance to help them establish career priorities before making such a major step. Once the decision is made there may be no turning back, bitterness and unhappiness may result, divorce or separation may follow and employers find themselves with unhappy, less productive employees. Counselling may help to resolve employees' and spouses' problems before they become disastrous.

Problem: career not enhanced by move
If employees themselves do not perceive the new job offered to them as being a valuable step forward they may refuse to move. Employers need to consider carefully whether the move really is necessary and, if not, relocation would not be required and money saved. If, however, the job is in the best interest of the employee, it may be necessary to provide counselling to find out why the

employee disagrees. Career counselling may be required from a third party specialist to establish the employee's priorities and career choices for the future.

Rather than selecting employees for relocation who may then reject the move, one solution is for employers to advertise vacancies internally so that candidates self-select a relocation. This method has the drawback that employers may not attract their first choice into the new post.

In the case of a group move, employees face the prospect of moving to keep their jobs or leaving.

The need to create a mobility culture

Organizations which require mobility on a continuing basis need to create a company culture which encourages this. This chapter has so far taken a step by step approach to reducing employees' resistance to relocation through practical steps to encourage would-be refusers to move. Steps also need to be taken to encourage would-be movers to relocate. Emphasis must be placed on the importance to both the company and the individual of relocating.

Companies with repeated mobility requirements can develop a culture in line with this. Companies involved in one-off group move exercises face a more difficult problem, as employees are not expecting to move and may react negatively to any proposal to do so. The remainder of this chapter addresses the issue of developing a mobility culture as it relates to individual employee transfers. Chapter 5 examines the need for a mobility culture and how to create it for a group move.

Action to develop a mobility culture
Employees' contracts may contain a mobility clause but this is not enough in itself to show that they really are expected to move. When employees join the company, any need for mobility should be made clear and this should be reinforced at regular intervals. Any future potential mobility requirements and how employee's personal circumstances have changed could be discussed, for example, at annual appraisals. In this way, any request for mobility from the employer will not come as a major shock to the employee and employers are likely to have a better idea of whether the relocation will be accepted.

The Institute of Manpower Studies research into the relocation of managerial and professional staff[1] found that young employees are more likely to relocate than older workers. Having moved once, employees are more likely to move again. Although systematic mobility, namely mobility for its own sake, is time wasting, an evaluation of the need for mobility can indicate when moves would be beneficial to both the person and the company. A mobility audit is recommended by the Institute of Manpower Studies to review mobility patterns and improve information. Employee profiles help to identify who is likely to move and who is not.

Where possible employers should try to reduce their demand for mobility. This can be achieved by transfering staff, if possible, within regions rather than between them to reduce the need to move home. Encouraging employees to live in a central location to company sites may also reduce the need to move home on transfer.

The Institute of Manpower Studies also recommends that employers establish clear managerial authority on relocation, improve administration, and review incentives and financial assistance for movers.

Communication is the key to developing a mobility culture. An open management style with regard to mobility encourages those who are willing to relocate, and appears honest and fair to those who may not be able to move. It also enables employers to identify shortcomings in policy and practice and to put these right before experiencing employee resistance to relocation.

References

1 INSTITUTE OF MANPOWER STUDIES. *Relocating managers and professional staff – IMS report No. 139.* Brighton, Institute of Manpower Studies. 1987.

2 INDUSTRIAL RELATIONS REVIEW AND REPORT. 'Relocation survey 1: background and trends'. *Industrial Relations Review and Report.* No. 432, January 1989. pp. 6–11.

3 MERRILL LYNCH RELOCATION MANAGEMENT INTERNATIONAL LTD. *Fourth annual study of employee relocation policies among UK companies.* London, Merrill Lynch Relocation Management International Ltd., 1987.

4 BEAUMONT, STELLA. 'Why today's workers are on the move'. *Personnel Management.* Vol. 21, No. 4, April 1989. pp. 42–46.

5 PHH HOMEQUITY LTD. *Report on a study on employee mobility.* Swindon, PHH Homequity Ltd., 1987.

6 CBI EMPLOYEE RELOCATION COUNCIL. *Survey of domestic and international relocation policies.* London, CBI Employee Relocation Council. February 1989.
7 DEPARTMENT OF GEOGRAPHY, UNIVERSITY OF GLASGOW. 'The geography of quality of life'. *Department of Geography, University of Glasgow.* Occasional paper No. 22, 1988.
8 ROGERSON, R., MORRIS, A., FINDLAY, A. and PADDISON, R. *Quality of life in Britain's intermediate cities.* Glasgow quality of life group, University of Glasgow, 1989.
9 MUNTON, TONY. 'Education concerns'. *Relocation News.* No. 10, April 1989. pp. 3–5.
10 SHORTLAND, SUE. 'Spouses and relocation'. *Education and Social Issues Workshop.* CBI Employee Relocation Council. September 1987. pp. 60–80.
11 CBI EMPLOYEE RELOCATION COUNCIL. *Survey on spouses/partners and domestic assignments Volume I.* London, CBI Employee Relocation Council, 1990.

2

The relocation allowances package – what to pay

Although companies can take a social approach to relocation by providing support to reduce employee's anxieties about the move, the financial package remains the backbone of the assistance given.

This chapter examines the elements of typical relocation packages in various industry groups, looking particularly at the direct and indirect costs of moving (such as fees and disturbance payments), bridging loans and temporary accommodation payments made when purchase and sale do not coincide, and at additional housing cost allowances. It covers rented and purchased properties and the levels of help given to new staff and existing employees transferred at company request.

Eligibility and assistance available

Formal relocation policies provide a wealth of detail on the assistance that may be available to a relocating staff member and/or a recruit but eligibility for such assistance is more often than not discretionary. Relocation policies may state that employees have to have been living over a certain distance from their new place of work (usually 20 or 30 miles) and that relocating significantly reduces their journey time. Policies may require that employees' new homes are within a certain radius of their work location (around 20 or 25 miles is usual). To be eligible for the allowances package, employees must usually undertake to complete the move within six months of starting their job in the new location, although policies are increasingly showing flexibility on this issue to accommodate the needs of employees with school-age children.

Individual elements of the allowances package may themselves be discretionary, such as the availability of bridging finance and/or the use of a guaranteed house price scheme.

New recruits' relocation allowances packages are often less well defined than those of existing staff. Often only senior or key recruits qualify for benefits and then only at managerial or director discretion.

Key items
The relocation allowances package can be broken down into six main categories. These are:

- the direct costs associated with a relocation exercise
- the indirect costs or disturbance allowances paid
- costs incurred when purchases and sales do not coincide, including bridging loans, guaranteed sale price schemes and temporary accommodation
- expenses incurred through commuting, househunting and on moving day
- losses incurred through moving including London weighting and loss of a spouse's income
- the increased cost of accommodation on moving home.

Relocation allowances policies also usually contain a section on repayment should the employee leave the organization within a set period after the relocation has taken place and the allowances have been paid.

Direct costs

It is usual practice for companies to reimburse the direct costs incurred by employees when they move house. These may include:

- estate agent's fees
- advertising costs
- auctioneer's charges
- solicitor's fees
- stamp duty
- land registry fees
- search fees
- other solicitor's disbursements
- cost of arrangement/disposal of lease
- tenancy fees
- mortgage arrangement/redemption fees

- mortgage guarantee premia
- building society valuation fee
- private survey fee
- cost of disconnecting/reconnecting utilities (if not covered by the disturbance allowance)
- removal expenses and insurance
- storage charges and insurance
- gratuities
- insurance cover and rates on unsold property
- travel costs to return to old property for maintenance purposes.

First time buyers and those moving to and from rented accommodation receive the appropriate payments. New recruits and existing staff generally receive similar treatment under this section of the relocation allowances policy.

However, to contain costs, organizations are increasingly putting limits on the payment of direct costs or asking to see quotations before any payments are authorized. For instance, percentage or cash limits may be set on the reimbursement of solicitors' fees. At Rank Xerox Ltd, International Headquarters, legal fees are reimbursed to a maximum of 0.5 per cent of the sale price and 0.5 per cent of the purchase price with the exception of Scotland where 1 per cent maximum per transaction applies except for disbursements. At W H Smith, solicitors' fees are subject to a maximum of 0.55 per cent of sale and purchase price excluding VAT. Cornhill Insurance Group reimburses stamp duty but only for the first £175,000 of the new property.

In the main, companies pay the estate agent's charge in full – although there are exceptions: one firm in the insurance sector only pays two thirds. Cash limits are often placed on the reimbursement of advertising costs: a limit of £300 applies at Courtaulds for example.

The payment of survey fees varies widely between organizations. Some pay only one building society valuation survey while others pay for this plus one or two private surveys. Limits are usually placed on how much reimbursement is given for private surveys; £200 or £300 per survey is the norm.

Rather than placing cash or percentage limits on the payment of fees, companies can control costs by insisting that employees obtain quotations first. It is usual practice for employees to have to supply two or three quotations for removals and storage, with the employer authorizing payment for the lowest. Some organizations, however, require quotes from other service companies as well, for instance estate agents and solicitors. The Automobile Association, for example, requires three quotes from estate agents.

When companies reimburse storage charges, limits are usually attached to the length of time that goods may be left in store at the company's expense, with three or six months being usual practice.

Also to control costs, some organizations stipulate that their own services – for instance their legal departments – be used wherever possible. This is the case at Bradford and Bingley Building Society and Cornhill Insurance. Alternatively, the company may suggest the use of a company-nominated solicitor or reimburse fees up to the level charged by that company-nominated solicitor.

Not all house purchases go smoothly and a few policies make provision for the payment of the additional costs incurred by an employee through an abortive purchase. If the employee has not sold the old home before moving into the new one, two sets of running costs have to be met. A few companies assist with these payments, e.g. Pirelli General and Reckitt & Colman. Limits may be placed, however, on the length of time that the firm will pay these costs, for instance after six months at Reckitt & Colman the position is reviewed.

Disturbance allowances

When employees move home they incur not only direct costs such as fees and removal charges but indirect costs as well. These include the cost of refitting/cleaning carpets and curtains or possibly buying these items new, disconnecting and reconnecting utilities, losses on season tickets, club fees, unexpired subscriptions, school fees, telephone rentals and so on. To compensate employees for these and other sundry items, firms usually pay a disturbance allowance.

Disturbance allowances take many forms. They may be given as a flat-rate sum, as a percentage of salary or as a number of months' salary. Their levels are usually related to the employee's own circumstances and, therefore, may vary according to the employee's grade at work, whether or not the property is owner-occupied or rented, whether the employee is married, has children or is single. Disturbance payments may even be related to the items necessary in the new property. New recruits and existing employees usually receive different treatment as far as disturbance is concerned.

The levels of payment vary widely – from just a few hundred pounds to several thousand pounds. Despite Inland Revenue guideline figures on the level of tax-free assistance which may be given, some companies have achieved better deals with their local tax inspectors with the result that there is a wide range of tax-free payments between organizations.

Certain industry groups (notably finance) pay two separate disturbance payments. Generally, one of these is tax-free, the other taxable. Others (principally the public sector) pay either one or two disturbance payments and then pay for incidental items on top.

On the administration side, some companies pay allowances against receipts; others pay the full allowance as stated in the policy but ask employees to keep receipts; and some do not require any bills at all.

Policies and practice on disturbance are diverse. The following table gives examples.

Table 1
Disturbance allowances

Organization	Disturbance
	Flat rate
Bournemouth Borough Council	Maximum of £225, against receipts. Tax-free.
Co-operative Insurance Society	£850. Tax-free.
Essex County Council	Maximum of £285. Tax-free.
Legal & General Group	Maximum of £2,233, against receipts. Tax-free.
Pirelli General	Up to £1,200. Existing staff, homeowners only. Tax-free.
	Percentage of salary
J Bibby & Sons	10% of basic salary. Minimum of £1,000, maximum of £3,000. Tax-free.

Crosfield Electronics	10% of basic salary. Discretionary for new recruits. Tax-free.
Pilkington	12½% of salary. Existing staff only. Partially taxable.
Rumbelows	Up to 10% of basic salary, against receipts. Existing staff only. Tax-free.

Number of months' salary

Armstrong World Industries	1 month's salary. Minimum of £600. Existing employees only. Tax-free.
Owen Owen	Up to 1 month's gross salary. Tax-free.
G D Searle	1 month's salary. Existing staff only. Tax-free.

Personal circumstances

Allied Dunbar	10% of salary. Existing staff. £150 for new recruits moving from rented to rented: 1 month's salary plus £150 for first time buyers; 1 month's salary for owner-occupiers. Tax-free.
Courtaulds	$\frac{1}{6}$ of annual salary: existing staff with resident dependants. $\frac{1}{12}$ of annual salary: existing staff without resident dependants. Partially taxable.
General Accident	6% of house price or £2,000 whichever is lower, against receipts. Special arrangements for those in rented accommodation. Tax-free.
Fisons	Up to £2,500 or £4,000: existing staff moved on promotion. Up to £2,500 or £4,000 plus £480 (discretionary): existing staff moved without promotion. Discretionary up to £2,500 or £4,000: new recruits. Tax-free.
London & Manchester Assurance	£1,399. Householders £495. Non-householders.
Optical Fibres	15% of salary. Maximum of £400 if not a householder. Partially taxable.
Reckitt & Colman	Either 15% of annual gross salary

	in new appointment or tax-free sum whichever is greater. £1,973 – married employee. £1,207 – single employee. Allowances in excess of tax-free sums above are taxable.
Sun Life Assurance	10% of scale mid-point of employee's new grade. Tax-free.
Surrey County Council	Up to £575 (single staff) or £950 (married). Tax-free.
Tate & Lyle	10% of basic salary plus 1% for each child or dependent relative (excluding spouse) to 15% maximum. Overall cash limits of £1,000 minimum, £3,500 maximum. Allowance reduced by 50% if moves involve rented accommodation. New and existing staff. Partially taxable.
Unigate	2 months' salary, receipts required for ⅔ of the allowance. Existing and new staff, homeowners. 10% of salary. Existing and new staff, non-homeowners.
Bank of Scotland	**Two payments** Up to £1,725 or £1,900 according to grade, against receipts. Householders. Tax-free. Plus 10% of salary. Householders and non-householders. Taxable.
Burmah Oil Trading	£1,910. Partially taxable. Plus 5% of salary. Taxable. Existing employees only.
Cornhill Insurance	10% of new basic salary or £1,500 whichever is greater. Tax-free subject to Inland Revenue limits. Plus 10% of new basic salary or £1,500 whichever is greater. Taxable. Existing employees only.
Debenhams	10% of new basic salary. Maximum £2,500. Tax-free. Plus 50% of the above if sale and purchase are completed within 3

	months of appointment date. Taxable. New and existing staff.
Midland Bank	Costs paid against receipts. Tax-free. Plus 15% of salary for staff with dependants or 10% of salary for staff without dependants. Only 50% of this allowance paid if moves involve rented accommodation or parental home. Minimum and maximum cash limits applied. Taxable.
Rhône-Poulenc	£1,973 for married staff; £1,207 for single staff. Tax-free. Plus 10% of salary. Taxable. Existing staff.
Royal Bank of Scotland	Up to £1,885 or £2,042 according to grade. Tax-free. Plus 10% of basic salary at date of transfer – minimum £1,035 – taxable.

Additional expenses

The Post Office	Transfer grant: £1,973 married employees with children. £1,580 married employees. £475 single employees. Tax-free. Plus for single employees – £732 householders; £366 for those moving involving rented accommodation; £54 for those moving to and from a single unfurnished room. Tax-free. Plus telephone installation costs (if employee had a telephone in the old home), cost of installing TV aerial, dishwasher and washing machine plus losses on school fees and season tickets. Existing staff only.
UKAEA	£1,973 married employees with children. £1,580 married employees. £475 single employees. Tax-free. Plus for single employees – £732 householders; £366 for those moving involving rented accommodation; £54 for those moving to and from a single

unfurnished room. Tax-free. Plus
installation costs for washing
machines and dishwashers, cost
of installing a telephone (if
employee had a telephone in the
old home), cost of installing a TV
aerial, cost of double payment of
school fees for one term. Existing
staff only.

Source: CBI Employee Relocation Council[1] and Industrial Relations
Services.[2]

School uniforms
Although, in the main, disturbance allowances usually include a
sum to cover additional expenses on school uniforms, a few firms
pay for this as a separate item under the disturbance section of
their policies. School fees may also be listed separately. For
example at Courtaulds, besides their disturbance allowance,
employees also receive reimbursement for new school uniforms
and school fees paid which are forfeited through the move. London
and Manchester Assurance pays a maximum uniform allowance
of £56.55 per child and Sun Life Assurance pays £125 if the child
is in primary education or £165 if in secondary education.

Bridging loans and guaranteed sale price schemes

When the sale and purchase of property do not coincide, employees
may need bridging finance to purchase their new homes. Over
three-quarters of organizations with formal relocation policies
offer bridging loans and/or the use of a guaranteed sale price
scheme. For example, in an Industrial Relations Services[2] survey
of 55 organizations, 41 provided bridging finance and in a CBI
Employee Relocation Council[1] survey of 80 companies, around 85
per cent offered either bridging finance or a guaranteed sale price
scheme.

New staff are less likely to receive bridging finance than existing
employees. However, as recruitment practice becomes more competitive employers are improving their relocation allowances packages for recruits in a bid to attract them.

There is little difference in the provision of bridging facilities by
industry group, although it is less common in local government
than elsewhere.

Guaranteed sale price schemes via third party companies are rare for new recruits, although some very senior staff and key specialists may benefit from them. For example, Rhône-Poulenc offers a guaranteed sale price scheme to selected key new and existing staff.

Controlling and funding cost
The provision of bridging assistance is an expensive item in the relocation package. In early 1989, a £30,000 bridging loan at commercial interest rates, less tax relief, cost in the region of £1,700 for six months. The management fee charged by third party relocation management companies offering guaranteed sale price schemes is around the same figure, with any necessary bridging loan interest charged on top. And, of course, many employees have bridging loans in excess of £30,000.

Employers, therefore, usually take some steps to control bridging loan expenditure. The most common way is to lay down a time limit on how long employees can have a bridging loan paid for by their employers. Usually when interest-free bridging is offered it is for either three or six months, although occasionally it may be provided for as long as a year.

Some organizations only give bridging finance when certain criteria are met, namely that the employee asks a realistic price for the property and waits for a reasonable period for a prospective buyer; also that the employee does not over-commit himself/herself on the new property.

The main drawback with offering interest-free bridging finance lies in withdrawing it when the three or six month period is up. Employees often cannot afford to pay for bridging themselves. There is a tendency, therefore, for bridging to stretch on, with costs going out of control. In an effort to prevent this, employers may phase out bridging by charging employees a proportion of the cost of the loan and increase payment required as time goes on. Alternatively, organizations may combine the provision of a bridging loan with the use of a guaranteed sale price scheme or insist that a guaranteed sale price scheme operates either through the company itself or through a third party relocation management company.

In normal circumstances, an employee requiring bridging finance would arrange this through commercial sources and pay rates above mortgage interest levels. On relocation, employers either arrange this finance themselves (either from internal or external funds) and give the employee an interest-free loan or allow employees to arrange the financing and then compensate them. The latter may prove more expensive as generally companies can achieve lower cost bridging finance than employees.

Under a guaranteed sale price scheme run by the company, the employer buys the house (using internal or external resources to do this) and then sells it on to another buyer. Under a scheme run by a third party relocation management company, the third party firm buys the employee's property (using its own or external finances), the employer pays interest on the loan given to the employee and the third party firm sells the house on to the eventual buyer. An explanation of how a third party relocation management company guaranteed sale price scheme operates is given in Chapter 1 and the tax implications are explained in Chapter 4.

Employers providing bridging loans
The main problem with the provision of a bridging loan is the potential for run-away costs. Companies deal with this in a number of ways. The first is to ensure that independent valuations are carried out on the old property so that a realistic sale price can be determined. For example at the Automobile Association, interest-free bridging is available for six months but is subject to an independent valuation to establish the realistic selling price of the house. At BP, two valuations of the property are taken and an average is calculated. The bridging loan given – which is interest-free for six months – does not exceed this average or, in certain circumstances, the actual sale price.

At the Milk Marketing Board, bridging finance amounts to not less than 95 per cent of the valuation of the old home. At Cadbury Schweppes, interest-free bridging is given to existing employees only for three months and after this the company arranges for an independent valuation of the property before any extension of the interest-free period is granted.

To ensure that employees' bridging loans do not run on indefinitely, companies may insist that bridging finance is only available once contracts have been exchanged or that the contract for sale of the old property has been signed. For example, at Trusthouse Forte, interest-free bridging for up to three months is available only when the contract for the sale of the employee's property has been signed.

Companies may place limits on bridging loans. To ensure that employees do not borrow more from the company than would be lent by a building society to buy their new properties, Armstrong World Industries limits bridging loans to 3.3 times the employee's annual salary.

Once the time limit for bridging has been reached, some allowances policies state that employees have to start paying interest. At British Gas, for instance, the bridging loan is interest-free for three months and if the loan extends beyond this, interest is charged at base rate plus 1 per cent, with the maximum length of bridging being six months. Debenhams, too, charges 1 per cent over base rate on bridging loans after three months. At the Automobile Association, a penalty scheme comes into play after the six month interest-free period is up. Internally relocated employees receive a 2.5 per cent or 4 per cent mortgage subsidy as part of their employee benefits package. After six months of interest-free bridging, however, they cease to receive this benefit until the bridging loan is repaid. Externally relocated employees, to whom subsidies do not apply, are charged 2.5 per cent interest after the six month interest-free period and until the loan is redeemed.

Companies providing guaranteed sale price schemes
As an alternative to bridging finance, companies may run a guaranteed sale price scheme in which the employer or a third party buys the employee's house for an agreed guaranteed price based on the average of two or three independent valuations. The employee receives the money from this transaction to buy a new home and the employer or the third party has to sell on the property to its eventual buyer.

Companies operating such arrangements generally use a third party relocation management company, although a few companies – such as BP – run the scheme themselves.

When a guaranteed home sale scheme is used and employees must participate in it, employers have little option other than to pay the bridging loan interest until the old home is sold. The question that arises here is what happens when the home is sold either for more or for less than the guaranteed sale price offered to the employee. When the property sells for less, the employer makes up the shortfall. Usually, if the house sells for more than the guaranteed price, the employee receives this excess. However, there are some exceptions. At Reckitt & Colman, for example, under the relocation company's guaranteed price scheme, two valuations of the property are taken (three if the variation is more than 5 per cent). Based on this, the relocation company makes an offer to purchase the property from the employee. If the house sells for more than the offer price given to the employee, then the employee receives a share of the excess as follows: all of it if the house sells within three months of the employee receiving the offer price; three quarters within three to six months; half within six to nine months; one quarter within nine to 12 months; nil thereafter. At Rohm & Haas, if the property sells for more than the official valuation price, deductions from this profit are made for the cost of the loan.

Which to choose?

Rather than insisting that employees use a guaranteed price scheme, the majority of organizations with such arrangements allow employees to opt out. The question that arises here is should employees be offered bridging facilities if they have chosen not to use the guaranteed home sale scheme and, if so, on what terms?

Usually, if employees opt out of a guaranteed home sale scheme it is because they believe that the guaranteed price offered is too low and that they can sell their home for more. One way to avoid providing a company bridging loan is to build a degree of flexibility into the guaranteed sale price scheme so that employees have a limited opportunity to gain a better price for their homes. For example, at the Milk Marketing Board, a home sale support scheme operates as well as a bridging finance scheme. Under the former, which is voluntary, two valuations of the employee's home are taken (three if the first two differ by more than 8 per cent). These are averaged and the house is then offered for sale for 30 days at not more than 10 per cent above the average valuation. If the house is not sold, it may then be offered for sale for a further 60 days at not more than 5 per cent above the average valuation. However, offers equal to the valuation have to be accepted. If the property is not sold after 90 days, the company guarantees a loan equal to its valuation, less 5 per cent and pays interest (net of tax). Subsequently, any offers of 95 per cent valuation or above must be accepted and the loan cleared. If offers are below 95 per cent of the valuation, the company decides whether to instruct the employee to accept or not and if so, any shortfall is paid by the company.

If employees do not wish to participate in the guaranteed sale price scheme at all, companies do usually provide some alternative bridging finance scheme. Terms are generally much stricter in such circumstances than under bridging loan schemes where no alternative guaranteed sale price scheme is available.

Loss on purchase price
If an employee is asked to relocate in a depressed or falling market or if there is a catastrophic collapse of house prices in a particular locality, the employee may receive less for the house than he or she paid for it.

If property prices are falling throughout the country there is less of a case for employers to make up employees' loss on purchase price. If, however, house prices collapse in one place only (the Aberdeen house price crash is well known) employees may expect their companies to make good their losses on the basis that if it were not for relocation, they would sit tight and wait for prices to rise before selling. Many oil companies and some others reimburse employees for actual loss on purchase price in such circumstances with compensation based on independent valuations of the property.

No assistance is given, however, to compensate for any hypothetical loss of benefit – if for instance, employees might have benefited from an increase in house prices had they not been relocated to an area where house prices subsequently crashed.

Loss on sale
If employees are forced through relocation to sell quickly (for example if no bridging finance is available), they may have to lower their price below the market rate for houses in the area. In some companies, compensation is given for loss on sale based on the difference between the actual selling price and the market value of the house as determined by independent valuations.

More usually, however, loss on sale policies operate through guaranteed sale price schemes, under which employers are effectively trading unknown bridging loan interest for a known cash loss to reduce costs for the company.

Temporary accommodation

When the sale and purchase of property do not coincide, temporary accommodation may be required. If the old home has not been sold before the employee is expected to take up the new job, the company may have to pay temporary accommodation costs for the employee in the new location while the family remains behind. Alternatively, if the old home is sold before the new home has been bought, then the employee and the family will all need to live in temporary accommodation in the new area.

Employee only
When the employee is separated from the family, it is usual for companies to meet temporary accommodation and subsistence costs for five nights a week and pay for employees' travelling costs home at weekends.

Temporary accommodation policies may contain a wealth of detail on items for which the company is prepared to pay. Bed, breakfast and evening meal are the norm; alcoholic drinks, newspapers, laundry and telephone calls are usually excluded. In general, organizations pay these expenses for a maximum of 13 weeks/three months, although a few make provision for longer periods (for up to six months plus weekend travel home at British Gas and at Legal & General).

Limits may be placed on the maximum amount of money that employees can spend on accommodation and subsistence. At London & Manchester Assurance, for example, three months' temporary accommodation costs are met to a maximum of £41.40 subsistence per night, plus second class rail fares. At the Milk Marketing Board, guideline figures for three months' temporary accommodation range from £22 to £29 per day (depending on the employee's grade) for moves to the provinces or between £29 and £33 per day for moves into London.

As an alternative to reimbursing hotel and subsistence costs, a few organizations pay a weekly allowance. The Automobile Association pays an accommodation allowance for up to 24 weeks, ranging from £36 to £50 per week depending on the employee's grade and location. Rediffusion Simulation pays between £50 and £75 per week, depending on grade, for up to 26 weeks.

Another approach is for employers to pay hotel costs for a short period, followed by a payment towards lodging in 'digs'. At Pirelli General, for example, hotel expenses are paid for six weeks followed by expenses for digs for a further 10 weeks.

Temporary accommodation policies sometimes offer an employee the choice between a relatively short period of hotel accommodation or a longer period in cheaper accommodation, rented property or digs. At Rhône-Poulenc employees can have a maximum of 12 weeks' hotel accommodation, or guest house accommodation for up to 26 weeks, or bed and breakfast accommodation or rent for a furnished flat for up to 39 weeks. If company accommodation is available, employees would normally be expected to use this.

Occasionally, policies make reference to employees staying with friends or relations instead of living in temporary accommodation. If this is the case the company usually makes a contribution towards their living expenses.

Some policies draw a distinction between homeowners and non-homeowners as far as allowable periods of temporary accommodation are concerned. For example, at British Aerospace, a subsistence allowance for temporary accommodation may be paid for up to six months for those who are moving home, whereas the limit is 13 weeks for those who simply have to find new permanent digs. At 3M, employees moving from unfurnished accommodation or those who have dependants living with them, receive payment of hotel expenses for up to three months, plus weekend travel home. Employees moving from rented furnished accommodation or from their parents' home receive hotel expenses for one month. And, at the Royal Bank of Scotland, householders receive out-of-pocket expenses for up to six months, first-time buyers for up to three months and non-householders for up to four weeks.

To control costs, policies may restrict the number of paid visits employees may take to go home at weekends. At Air Products, fares home are paid in lieu of accommodation. If the cost of fares exceeds two days' *per diem* allowance, the company pays fares for the first two weekends and for alternate weekends thereafter.

The family

If the family has sold the old home and requires temporary accommodation in the new area, provision is generally made by companies to pay for this. However, this increases company costs and so stricter limits are usually placed on how long the family can continue this at the firm's expense. At Rhône-Poulenc employees on their own may stay in a hotel for up to 12 weeks; if they are accompanied by their families, the limit is reduced by a third to eight weeks.

While the family is living in temporary accommodation, having sold its old home, it follows that it is saving money because it is no longer meeting the usual household bills (mortgage, rates, utilities, etc). To help reduce costs, a few companies require the employee and family to make a contribution towards the temporary accommodation costs equivalent to their commitments at the old location. Debenhams, for example, requires this.

Because of the expense involved, some organizations' relocation policies do not make any provision to pay temporary accommodation costs incurred by spouses and children.

Children taking exams
Employees with children who are approaching crucial examinations may wish them to remain in the old location to complete their courses of study. This may well result in either the relocation of the employee being delayed or the family being separated for a period. In the latter case, temporary accommodation may be required. But only a few policies make provision for this.

At Unilever, if employees have children who are taking critical examinations (e.g. GCSE or 'A' levels), the company offers some financial assistance to help pay for the costs which arise if the child is not relocated. Payment may take one of two forms. The first option – which is partly taxable – provides assistance with accommodation costs for up to one year for each child affected, up to a maximum of £1,000 per year per child (or in proportion for a part year). The second option is for the family to remain in the old location until the completion of the examination. Payment given is for one year's temporary accommodation for the manager in the new location, plus an appropriate meal allowance.

The United Kingdom Atomic Energy Authority (UKAEA) and the Post Office also make provision for a child to stay in lodgings for educational reasons for up to five full academic terms. The Post Office pays £9.35 per week and UKAEA pays half board and lodging costs up to £15.65 per week.

Commuting

Commuting allowances may be paid to employees who choose to commute to the new location rather than relocate or to those who prefer to commute rather than stay in temporary accommodation while they await completion of their house purchase in the new location.

At BP, existing staff who qualify for a full house move but prefer to commute instead, receive reasonable additional commuting costs for daily travel for four years. The amount paid is based on annual second class season tickets and is grossed up for tax and National

Insurance Contributions (NIC). The Children's Society meets additional travelling costs for four years and these are based on second class rail/bus fares or current car mileage allowances. At one major company in the service industry, established employees whose new job location involves significant additional travel but is within commuting distance, receive a travel subsidy based on their additional travelling costs. The subsidy is reduced from 100 per cent in year one, to 66 per cent in year two and to 33 per cent in year three.

At Legal & General Group, excess travel costs are met if no move of home is necessary. These are paid for two and a half years, reassessed each 12 months in the light of increasing cost of travel. The allowance is grossed up for tax and NIC. At Gallaher, additional travelling expenses are reimbursed by the company for one year if the employee does not move house.

Employees opting to commute rather than stay in temporary accommodation have their excess travel costs paid for three months at the Milk Marketing Board and Woolworths and for 13 weeks at Rank Xerox Ltd, International Headquarters. At the United Kingdom Atomic Energy Authority, excess travel costs are met in lieu of lodging and subsistence allowances and are normally payable for 13 weeks.

Househunting and removal

Virtually all relocation allowances policies make some reference to househunting. It can prove to be a time consuming and costly business and so policies generally state how many househunting trips are allowable at company expense, who can go, when they can be made (that is, at weekends or in the company's time) and whether paid leave is granted. It is usual practice for companies to meet the expenses incurred by the employee and spouse for either two or three househunting visits with hotel, meal and travel expenses being reimbursed against receipts. Non-homeowners may be granted less time or a lower allowance than homeowners for househunting.

Although it is less common, some relocation policies make provision for children to accompany their parents while househunting (for example at Asda Stores). Du Pont also pays for children to accompany their parents on househunting trips or for babysitters'/childminders' expenses if parents prefer to leave their children at home. Asda Stores' policy makes provision for an extra couple of househunting trips at company expense if the first house purchase falls through.

Rather than stipulating how many househunting trips are made at company expense, a few firms have adopted a different approach. At Sun Life Assurance Society, for example, employees are told how much money they can spend on househunting and it is up to them how to spend it. At Sun Life, the househunting allowance is paid in advance as a lump sum, with the amount depending on individual circumstances. As an example, a married employee moving from London to Bristol would have received £660 in 1989 made up as follows: hotels – 14 nights at £30 = £420; return fares (two trips) – four at £35 each = £140; dependent children – two at £50 each = £100.

Paid time off for househunting varies from one or two days to five days. Table 2 gives some examples of househunting policies.

Removal
It is usual for companies to pay for the employee and family's travelling and subsistence expenses on removal day. Some employers give one or two days' paid leave.

London weighting

When relocated at company request, employees may find that they no longer qualify for London weighting or area allowances.

Relocation allowances policies may compensate for this, especially if the move is the result of a company head office relocation exercise away from the capital. In the main, allowances are gradually phased out over three or four years. One-off buy outs of area allowances are rare. However, as with the other elements of the allowances policy, practice is diverse. At the Post Office, for instance, a taxable lump sum dispersal allowance is paid to those moving from the inner London pay area to the outer London pay area and to those moving from either inner or the outer London into the national pay area. It is paid in the form of a loan which is reduced by 20 per cent a year and is written off within five years. Should the employee leave within that time, any balance outstanding is repayable.

Table 2
Househunting

Organization	Househunting
Armstrong World Industries	Up to 3 visits (employee and spouse). Accommodation and travel costs paid (return fares or car mileage allowance).
BASF Coatings & Inks Ltd	Up to 4 nights' accommodation (employee and family) plus petrol or second class fares.
Debenhams	Up to 3 weekend visits by family.
Lloyds Bowmaker	Up to 2 visits of up to 2 nights each (employee and spouse). 3 days' leave given. Expenses are met for children to accompany parents but only when no other arrangement is possible.
Rank Xerox Ltd, International Headquarters	2 days' paid leave, in addition to holiday entitlement. Travel costs reimbursed. 2 nights' bed & breakfast plus £20 each for two days for meals against receipts. Hire car plus petrol in new location to a maximum of 4 days.
The Wellcome Foundation	3 visits (employee and family). Bed and breakfast costs paid plus second class fares.

Source: CBI Employee Relocation Council.[1]

At the Children's Society, London weighting and fringe allowances continue for four years. They are paid to employees who relocate and to those who choose to commute to the new location instead. Thereafter, area allowances are paid at the applicable rate. One company in business services gives a taxable payment of one year's London weighting to those employees relocating out of the capital.

Spouse's income compensation

Very few relocation allowances policies provide financial compensation to employees' spouses who lose their jobs on relocation. In one example, the company pays up to two months' gross loss of income to spouses of relocated senior managers and up to one month's gross loss of income to the spouses of other relocated managers. This compensation is taxable and is limited to the maximum of the employee's salary. Another organization reimburses the employee with the gross difference between the spouse's loss of earnings and unemployment benefit (if any) for six months or until the spouse finds employment, whichever is the sooner.

High cost housing area assistance

Staff moving into a high cost housing area face the additional financial burden of increased mortgage repayments or higher rents. As a result, companies usually provide some assistance in the form of a loan, a subsidized mortgage facility or an additional housing cost allowance. Other forms of assistance include equity sharing, equity mortgages, deferred interest loan arrangements and two homes allowances schemes. These are dealt with in greater detail in the next chapter.

Relocation allowances policies rarely contain clauses covering equity financing arrangements. In the main, additional housing cost allowance schemes provide the most common method of assistance, with loans and subsidized mortgage facilities offered mainly in the banking and finance sector. Assistance with additional housing costs is usually restricted to existing staff who are moved at company request, and is not given to new staff. This is because there are tax advantages for existing staff – provided that the payments they receive are in keeping with Inland Revenue guidelines (Extra-Statutory Concession A67), while no such tax benefits apply to relocated recruits. However, as recruitment packages become more competitive, an increasing number of organizations may offer additional housing cost allowances to new employees.

Loans and mortgage subsidies
Cheap loans and mortgages are a common benefit in the finance sector, although service and/or age criteria are usually applied before they are granted. Some other organizations provide similar

assistance to their employees – either to help them cope with their mortgage repayments generally or to assist them specifically if they are relocated into a high price area. Loans may be interest-free or at low interest rates. British Steel has a scheme under which employees who cannot bridge the gap in house prices through an increased mortgage may be granted an interest-free loan, repayable over 10 years.

There are a number of loan schemes available to relocating employees at Du Pont (UK) Ltd, including:

- A lease acquisition loan for non-homeowners (up to £3,000 or actual expenses, whichever is the lower, repayable on subsequent transfer or on leaving the company);
- A housing expense loan for non-homeowners (if costs exceed half a month's salary – up to £3,000 or actual expenses, whichever is the lower, repayable within five years);
- An equity loan (interest-free for six months) to enable the deposit to be paid on the new house (rarely used, however, as money is usually drawn down from a bridging facility to cover the deposit);
- A house purchase assistance loan under which a loan is provided by the company at current building society rate of interest. Interest only is paid by the employee for the first three years and capital plus interest over the next 10 years.

A maximum of £15,000 may be borrowed by the employee under the equity loan and house purchase assistance loan.

Loans and mortgage subsidies may be related to the area into which the employee is asked to move. At the Post Office, for example, employees aged over 18 with two years' service may receive an interest-free loan, repayable over 10 years (with the possibility of deferring repayment by two years) of £6,500 or six months' gross salary (whichever is greater) for moves into London or £5,000 or six months' gross salary (whichever is greater) for moves elsewhere.

At the Automobile Association, internally relocated management and staff moving into the South East may receive a mortgage subsidy of 4 per cent of the capital balance of their outstanding mortgage at the end of each tax year, while those moving elsewhere in the country receive a 2.5 per cent mortgage subsidy.

Under the Royal Bank of Scotland's loan scheme, staff who are relocated may borrow up to four times their salary to a maximum of £60,000 at 5 per cent interest. On moving to London or the South East, they may borrow five times their salary (including London weighting) again to a maximum of £60,000 at 5 per cent interest. Any further borrowing is at customer mortgage rates. For comparison, everywhere apart from London and the South East, normal staff borrowing is restricted to four times salary, with up to £30,000 at 5 per cent, with any excess at base rate up to £60,000 and thereafter at customer mortgage rates. In London and the South East the borrowing limit is five times salary including London weighting, with up to £50,000 at 5 per cent and any excess at customer mortgage rate.

Additional housing cost allowances
The main change to relocation allowances policies over the past few years has been the introduction of the additional housing cost allowance. This is also often referred to within relocation policies as an excess mortgage or excess rent allowance or as a mortgage subsidy scheme. Under these schemes, employers provide financial assistance towards employees' additional mortgage interest charges and other additional costs, such as rates and house insurance (or rent), when they relocate into an area of high cost housing.

Employers' schemes vary but the basic principle is that employees are compensated for additional mortgage interest incurred with the payments tapering down over a number of years. The tapering arrangement may be quite short (for example two or three years) or as long as nine years in the Civil Service and the United Kingdom Atomic Energy Authority. However, the average length is around five years.

The Inland Revenue's Extra-Statutory Concession A67 provides details of the tax-free maximum payment allowable to existing employees. This figure varies from time to time, taking into account interest rate changes, etc. As and when the tax-free maximum additional housing cost allowance changes, employees who move on or after the date of the change receive the new increased/decreased figure. Employees already receiving additional housing cost allowances are unaffected by the new tax-free maximum.

Many companies simply follow the Inland Revenue guidelines and limit their payment to the tax-free maximum in force on the date that the employee moves. A few, however, pay more than this figure or vary their payments as interest rates rise or fall.

Practice varies with regard to payment of tax. In the main, the employee is responsible for paying income tax on any sums received over and above the Inland Revenue maximum. However, in a few companies the relocation allowances policy states that the employer grosses up all monies received by the employee or grosses up the payment to some extent (for example at 3M and Unilever). At Unilever, the 'excess mortgage interest allowance' as it is known, is adjusted twice a year to reflect interest rate changes of plus or minus 1 per cent, while at British Gas the interest rate is set once a year and revised during the year if building society rates alter by plus or minus 1.5 per cent.

The payment of the additional housing cost allowance is based on the difference in house prices between the old and the new areas and the cost of financing this difference.

Practice on establishing house price differences varies considerably. Some firms use established house price data as published regularly by building societies such as the Halifax and the Nationwide Anglia; others use relocation consultants/valuers to establish house price differentials; others use an index, either drawn up by the company itself or by an outside source, to multiply house prices by a factor either up or down between the low and high cost areas.

Employees naturally wish to trade up when they move house. Policies, however, do not make provision for this, with house price calculations and therefore payments, based only on moves to houses of similar specification. If employees do trade up they, themselves, are responsible for any additional expenditure.

Even without trading up, it is possible for house price differences between regions to exceed the £30,000 maximum allowable by the Inland Revenue in its calculation of a tax-free maximum payment. Some policies compensate for greater house price differences (for instance to a maximum of £50,000 at 3M and £55,125 at Du Pont) with the associated income tax charge being paid either by the employer or the employee.

To prevent employees trying to borrow more money than they could comfortably repay, an increasing number of companies place limits on how much extra mortgage commitment an employee can take on.

Additional housing cost allowance schemes cease to be paid when employees leave their companies. At Gallaher, if employees decide to move house again of their own volition, the company subsidy may cease.

When employees move to and from low and high cost areas,

additional housing cost allowances are recalculated. Further details are given in the next chapter.

Repayment

Companies invest considerable sums of money in their employees on relocation, with some £7,000 to £10,000 being spent on direct, indirect and accommodation costs alone. Payments to employees to compensate them for moving into a high cost housing area can add up to £20,000 to the bill and any bridging facility given raises costs still further.

It is not surprising, therefore, to find companies trying to control costs through some form of repayment clause in the policy. Under this, employees repay all or part of their relocation expenses if they should leave their employer within a certain number of years after the relocation. It is common practice for employers to grant relocation expenses in the form of a loan which is written off if the employee stays for the required length of time and is repayable should the employee leave early.

About two-thirds of companies now have these clauses, although how they work varies widely in practice and is often discretionary. For example, the reason for leaving determines, in some instances, the requirement to repay part or all of the expenses. Generally, employers do not require repayment if the employee is made redundant. A few policies state that the company does not require repayment if employees resign through ill-health or if they retire or die, although firms do usually use discretion when implementing repayment requirements under these circumstances.

Service required after move
In general repayment terms apply to employees who leave within two years of the relocation. At Debenhams, repayment for both new and existing staff depends on service with the company as well as service after relocation. The precise date from when the repayment clause operates varies considerably from company to company: it may be taken as the date when the employee completes the purchase of the new house, from the date of taking up the new appointment, from the date of the last relocation payment being made and/or, in the case of a company move, from the date of the company's relocation to the new area.

In table 3, there are 15 company examples of repayment

requirements with associated periods of service ranging from less than one year to less than three years after the move.

A recent survey from Industrial Relations Services[3] indicates a degree of consistency between the length of the repayment clauses and industry group. It found, for instance, that in public services, clauses tend to operate over a three year period, with repayments required pro-rata to length of service after relocation. In food, drink and tobacco, two years is the average, while in the distribution and leisure, and engineering sectors one year or two years is usual. Repayment clauses, it finds, are less common in finance and general manufacturing.

Amount due

In the main, organizations apply a stepped scale of repayments corresponding with fixed periods of service after relocation. For example, at BASF Coatings and Inks Ltd, repayments are reduced by 25 per cent for each six months' service after the move. Another practice is to reduce repayments pro-rata to months of service. This is the case, for example, at W H Smith where repayments are reduced by $\frac{1}{24}$th for each complete month worked from appointment date to date of leaving.

Generally, employers seek to reclaim all or part of relocation expenses paid out in line with service after relocation. Some firms, however, only require repayment of expenditure made on certain items in the relocation policy (e.g. W H Smith and Unigate). At Asda Stores, the following relocation expenses must be repaid on a stepped repayment scale operating over two years: solicitor's fees; estate agent's fees; building society valuation fees and redemption charges; the cost of removal of effects; the disturbance allowance; and, if appropriate, the cost of disposing of rented accommodation.

The payment of interest on a bridging loan is an expensive item in the allowances package. Some firms, therefore, specifically mention that leavers must repay this. For example British Aerospace requires certain proportions to be repaid by anyone who resigns within specified periods after relocation. At Rohm & Haas, both new and existing staff who leave within 24 months of moving house may have to repay, pro-rata for each complete month worked, interest at 1 per cent over clearing bank base rate on any bridging loan.

Table 3
Repayment provisions

Organization	Repayment provisions
Automobile Association	Less than 2 years: repayment of all or part of the allowance (new and existing staff).
Air Products plc	Less than 12 months' service from date of last relocation payment: repayment required (new and existing staff, homeowners and non-homeowners, single and married staff).
BASF Coatings and Inks Ltd	Less than 2 years from date of move: 100% repayment during first six months; 75% repayment 6 to 12 months; 50% repayment during 1 to 2 years; nil if employee leaves after two years (new and existing staff).
Bradford and Bingley Building Society	Less than 2 years: repayment of the disturbance allowance in full during 1st year; repayment of 50% of the disturbance allowance during 2nd year (homeowners).
British Aerospace	Less than 2 years: repayment of 80% of the disturbance and resettlement allowances, and other relocation allowances and expenses during 1st year; 40% of the above during 2nd year; nil after 2nd year (new and existing employees). As above also for bridging loan interest for existing employees, but over 3 years (80%, 60%, 40%) for new employees, for whom this facility is only granted exceptionally.
British Gas	Less than 2 years: all payments must be repaid (new recruits only).
Cornhill Insurance Group	Less than 2 years: removal expenses including disturbance allowance are treated as an

	interest free loan, repayable if employee leaves within 2 years of date of appointment (new and existing staff).
Debenhams	Less than 2 years: employees with under 2 years' company service repay all direct costs and disturbance plus any outstanding bridging finance, plus interest if employee leaves within 12 months from the date of the move; 50% of the above costs are repayable if employee leaves between 12 and 24 months (new and existing staff, not redundancy). Less than 12 months: employees with over 2 years' company service repay 50% of the above costs if they leave within 12 months from date of the move (new and existing staff, not redundancy).
Legal & General Group	Less than 1 year: repayment in full.
Pirelli General plc	Less than 3 years: repayment of all or part of relocation allowances may be required.
Rhône-Poulenc	Less than 2 years: repayment of 75% of all expenses, including mortgage assistance during first year; 50% during 12 to 18 months; 25% during 18 months to 2 years; nil after 2 years (all employees – new and existing, homeowners and non-homeowners).
W H Smith	Less than 2 years: repayment, pro-rata, of the financial package excluding temporary accommodation, unsuccessful purchase costs and househunting costs, excludes leavers through ill-health, retirement and redundancy.

Unigate	Less than 12 months: repayment of disturbance allowance (new employees).
United Biscuits	Less than 1 year: repayment required if employee leaves voluntarily (new employees only).
Woolworths	Less than 18 months: all or part of relocation expenses may have to be repaid at company discretion (new and existing staff). Basis of repayment is $\frac{1}{18}$ of the total amounts paid for each month of the 18 month period which remains after the date of leaving.

Source: CBI Employee Relocation Council.[1]

One of the most expensive items in the relocation package – the payment made to employees relocating into high cost areas – is, however, often excluded from repayment clauses.

New staff
New staff often fare worse than existing employees when it comes to repaying their relocation expenses. Firms may impose repayment clauses on new employees while existing employees receive their relocation expenses with no such conditions attached (e.g. at British Gas and United Biscuits). Alternatively, new recruits may be subject to repayment clauses covering more items in the allowances package than existing staff or the timescale over which the repayment clause operates may be longer for recruits than for existing workers.

References

1 CBI EMPLOYEE RELOCATION COUNCIL. *Survey of domestic and international relocation policies*. London, CBI Employee Relocation Council, 1989.
2 INDUSTRIAL RELATIONS REVIEW AND REPORT. 'Relocation survey 4: scheme basics, bridging loans and disturbance allowances'. *Industrial Relations Review and Report*. No. 437, April 1989. pp. 6–14.

3 INDUSTRIAL RELATIONS REVIEW AND REPORT. 'Relocation survey 3: controlling costs, administration and eligibility'. *Industrial Relations Review and Report*. No. 436, March 1989, pp. 6–11.

3

How to overcome the North–South divide – moves to and from high cost areas

The relocation of staff from low house price areas into expensive ones and vice-versa is a particularly thorny problem for employers. This chapter examines the options for employers and how they can be operated in practice. It covers additional housing cost allowance schemes, two homes allowances, company houses, equity sharing, loans and mortgages, and shared ownership schemes through links with housing associations. The tax implications of these practical relocation solutions are covered in the next chapter. Moves between private and other rented housing are also considered in this chapter.

Additional housing cost allowance scheme

When employees are transferred to an area where the cost of accommodation is higher than before, employers generally make a contribution towards these extra costs under additional housing cost allowance schemes. These may also be known as excess mortgage, excess rent or mortgage subsidy schemes. Any payments made are regarded as non-taxable under Extra-Statutory Concession A67, provided that the payments are clearly linked to the ongoing cost of accommodation at the new location and that certain conditions are satisfied.

Virtually all employers' schemes follow the terms laid down in Extra-Statutory Concession A67 so that employees' payments are tax-free. The standard procedure is for payments to be related to the price or rental cost of housing in the new location, which is roughly equivalent to that owned or rented in the old location. In other words, employers' schemes do not fund trading up. Payments are restricted to outgoings of a revenue nature, not a capital nature. Schemes, therefore, aim to compensate for increased mortgage interest, rent, rates, ground rent, etc paid by the employee, taking into account any tax allowances which may be claimed. Employers' schemes operate over a fixed period of time – generally between four and nine years – and payments taper out as the years progress.

The total additional housing cost allowance is calculated by multiplying the difference between house prices of comparable housing in the old and new location by the average mortgage interest rate after tax relief, multiplied by the length of time for which assistance is available (i.e. the total length of the taper). The amounts payable in the Civil Service are applied by the Inland Revenue as a tax-free maximum to industry. Employers may pay more but for any excess over the Civil Service limit, the employee is taxed. As a result, the majority of companies limit their payments to the maximum payable under the Civil Service scheme. Only a few companies pay more and either gross up or let their employees pay the necessary tax. (Details of company practice are given in the previous chapter.)

The main difference in the operation of housing allowance schemes in industry as compared with the Civil Service is in the structure of the tapering arrangement. The Civil Service operates a nine year taper with the allowance paid in full in years one to five; then reducing to 80 per cent in year six; 60 per cent in year seven; 40 per cent in year eight; and 20 per cent in year nine. Companies often taper their allowances over five years, reducing them by 20 per cent a year – but all sorts of other variations occur.

The advantage of a short taper (three or four years) with payments front loaded, is that the employee does not suffer the initial high cost shock of the new mortgage. The disadvantage is that after a couple years, as payments taper down or cease, the cost may prove too high, especially if the employee's pay has not risen significantly. Also if the employee leaves the company, the employer's investment in that person has been lost. Consequently, many employers prefer to adopt a longer taper of between five and nine years. A few have tapering arrangements that are longer than those in the Civil Service (10 to 12 years).

A second difference lies in calculating the house price differential. In the Civil Service, until recently, use was made of the Halifax Building Society's house price data which gives prices of housing in various regions of the country according to postcode. Some companies use the same system, others rely on house price data from other building societies or relocation companies, or on independent valuations from valuers or estate agents. (The Civil

Service now uses data supplied by the Valuations Office.) Some companies have constructed indices of house prices and use a comparison of these to determine their additional housing cost allowances.

Employees relocating across the North–South divide may find that it suits their circumstances to move from rented to purchased property or vice-versa. Additional housing cost allowances may be paid on a tax-free basis under Extra-Statutory Concession A67 in such circumstances. However, few company relocation policies mention that additional housing cost allowances are paid when such a change of residence occurs. (It is more usual for companies to restrict additional housing cost allowances to those moving to and from owner-occupied property and to restrict so-called excess rent allowances to those relocating between rented accommodation).

However, at British Aerospace, an additional housing cost allowance is payable when employees move into a higher cost area with payments depending on ownership. The calculation of the allowance is as follows, based on comparable properties, with the definition of 'X' as the building society, or other lender's mortgage interest rate ruling at the date the employee occupies the new accommodation, less any allowable tax relief. For sale and purchase of freehold or leasehold property: the allowance is X per cent of the difference between the prices of the two properties or X per cent of the amount by which the new house price exceeds twice the employee's salary, whichever is the less.

For moves from rented accommodation to freehold/leasehold property: the allowance is calculated as the amount by which X per cent of the purchase price exceeds the annual rent of the previous accommodation or X per cent of the amount by which the purchase price exceeds twice salary, whichever is the less. For moves between rented accommodation: it is the difference between rent at the old and new accommodation or the amount by which rent at the new location exceeds 10 per cent of salary, whichever is the less. No allowance is paid when the annual sum of rent and rates of the new location is equal to, or less than, 10 per cent of salary. For moves from freehold/leasehold property to rented accommodation: the allowance is the amount by which rent at the new location exceeds mortgage interest at the old location, less any tax relief or the amount by which rent at the new location exceeds 10 per cent of salary, whichever is the less. No allowance is paid where the annual sum of rent and rates at the new location is equal to, or less than, 10 per cent of salary. In all cases salary is defined as basic annual income at new location. The additional annual costs, if any, of rates, insurance of the property (but not of its contents nor any mortgage guarantees), and ground rent (but not maintenance/service charges) are aggregated with the amount calculated above to determine the total amount of additional housing cost allowance. No change is made to the allowance if the cost of any of these individual items changes or if interest rates change. The allowance is paid in full in monthly instalments for two years and then it is reduced by one eighth of the original figure for each year, with no allowance paid after the ninth year. A maximum of £20,000 is payable under the scheme, which currently is all tax-free.

Multiple moves
When an employee is relocated more than once, this may affect entitlement to an additional housing cost allowance. Companies need to determine the fairest method of calculating the additional housing cost allowance for employees who have moved from a low cost area as their first location to a higher priced area and then on to a third location within the period of the allowance. A number of situations can arise: housing may be more expensive in the third location than in the first but less expensive than in the second; housing may be more expensive than in the second location or less expensive than in the first.

Employers have a number of options. Using the case of an employee who moves from a low price area to a very expensive region and then on to a less expensive location, employers could base their calculation on the difference in price between the second and third location, in which case the allowance would cease, because the third property is less expensive than the second. However, employees would find it difficult to pay their mortgages without any assistance because they have incurred higher repayments in the third location than in their original location. Alternatively, employers could base their calculation on the difference in price between the first and third properties and either start a new allowance afresh for the full period when the employee moves into the third property or pay this lower scale of allowance for the remainder of the term that the housing allowance would normally be provided.

In the second case, namely where the employee's third property is more expensive than the second property, which in turn is more costly than the original home, employers again have choices. One is to start the housing allowance afresh for the full term of the allowance when the employee moves into the third property, basing the allowance on the difference in price between the second and third properties, although this does not compensate the employee for the original uplift in housing costs on moving from the original first home to the second. Another option is to pay an enhanced allowance during the remainder of the term of the existing allowance, plus an allowance based on the difference in price between the second and the third properties for remainder of the term, based on the date when the employee moved into the third location.

In the third case, namely where the third location costs less than the first, it is reasonable for the allowance to cease altogether.

The majority of relocation policies state that the allowance is recalculated when the employee moves again. This is a vague statement and does not help employees to understand their eligibility for assistance. In practice, many companies treat individual cases on an *ad hoc* basis. However, some companies are more precise in the wording of their policies.

For example, British Gas pays an additional housing cost allowance, for moves to a higher cost work location, over a seven year period. If, during this period, the employee is again transferred to an even higher cost location, then the balance of the allowance payable for the original move is added to the allowance calculated for the subsequent move, and this total amount is spread over the seven year period, starting with the second move. If the subsequent move to a third location is to a medium cost location (i.e. higher cost than first location but lower than second) then the current notional value of a house in the first location, comparable to the current house in the second, is calculated and this is used to determine the cost of comparable property in the third place. The employee receives the recalculated allowance over a seven year period minus the period during which the allowance was paid for the first move. Should the employee not be entitled to a further allowance, the existing one continues until the date of sale of the property or six months from the date of transfer, whichever is the earlier.

At BP the additional housing cost allowance is paid over six years. If a further move occurs during that period and involves increased cost, allowance payments are made at the new level for a further period of six years. If the second move results in a relocation to a lower cost area, the allowance is reduced (or it could cease) from the date of the move for the remainder of the original six years.

At the Wellcome Foundation, the additional housing cost allowance operates over nine years. If the employee moves to a lower cost housing area, the allowance ceases but if a further move results in the employee living in an area where costs are intermediate, the allowance is recalculated to correspond with the new costs. Payment of the revised allowance begins with the second move (that is, to the third property) and is payable for the remainder of the original nine year period.

At Asda Stores, employees who take up a new appointment in a lower cost area cease to receive mortgage assistance, while those moving to a higher priced area have their payments adjusted appropriately. And at Dun & Bradstreet, if the employee relocates to a low cost area compared to the original location, the housing allowance – which is payable over five years – ceases or is reduced. If, on the other hand, the employee relocates a second time to another high cost area, the subsidy continues with the amount eligible for tax relief recalculated if necessary. If the employee relocates from a high cost area to a low cost area and is subsequently relocated back into an area equivalent to the original high cost area, the difference in house prices is calculated by comparing the fair market value of the property in the low cost area with the lesser of the valuation of a comparable property in the new area and the current valuation of the original property in the original high cost area.

Trading up
When an employee moves from a high priced area into a low cost region, the employee is likely to buy a larger sized property and so enjoy the benefits of a higher standard of living and, if the relocation involves a promotion, trading up is certain to occur.

On moving back into a high priced area, the employee is unlikely to be able to afford a similar type of property. Mortgage constraints restrict the employee's borrowing and, even if sufficient funds could be raised, repayments are likely to be very high. Employers need to consider what restrictions they should place on the calculation of the additional housing cost allowance if they are to ensure fair treatment to employees under such circumstances.

There are several schools of thought on this issue. The first is to tell employees that, if they do trade up when they move to a cheaper area, they will have their housing allowance in the future based on the style of a similar property to that which they owned in the original location. If, for instance, employees move from a two bedroomed house to a four bedroomed property in the low cost area, the housing allowance on their return could be based on the difference in price between either a two bedroomed property in both the cheap and expensive regions or on the difference in price between the first house when it was sold and a comparable house in the expensive area on return, thus ignoring the move to the second location. Alternatively, the employer could calculate the uplift in price of the old two bedroomed property during the period that the employee lived in the cheaper area and the uplift in price of the new property during this same period and base pay and allowance on the difference.

The opposite approach is to treat the moves as two separate transactions. Under this method, when employees move from a high cost to a low cost area they are free to trade up. When the company moves them again back into the high cost area, the housing allowance policy is based on moves from like to like property. Funded by the company's housing allowance scheme, employees are able to maintain a similar standard of housing to that enjoyed in the cheaper area.

There are two main problems with the latter approach. First, it is extremely costly for the company. Second, it may cause employee relations problems as the company has, in effect, assisted the employee in leap frogging over colleagues in terms of housing and lifestyle.

The problem with the former approach lies in employee expectations. Although employees expect to have to trade down to some degree, after two promotions they do not want to return to the same standard of housing that they owned before the two relocations took place. Nevertheless, employers are more likely to adopt this approach because it keeps costs down.

Employers should consider whether they really do need that particular employee at a different location and, if so, employees need to decide whether they can afford to accept the transfer on this basis. The answer to this dilemma may well lie in the career opportunities for the employee and whether the trading down is likely to be temporary. After promotion, an increased salary may enable the employee to trade up again at a later date.

Two homes allowances

Employees who have to make several moves during their careers across the so-called North–South divide may resist fully transferring from a high to a low cost area. They are likely to be concerned about how they could afford to return to a high priced area, especially if house prices are escalating there. The offer of an accommodation allowance or two homes allowance can enable employees either to rent or to buy a second property in the new location and keep their home in the high priced area.

Before considering the payment of such an allowance, it is important to analyse the career paths available to staff within the company. For example, the company may be structured as a strong central organization offering a full career structure with career movements by employees being to and from this centre via branches. Another possibility is for the company to consist of several centres, each with a full range of careers available with career moves being both within and between centres.

In the first instance, it may prove appropriate to offer a two homes allowance, because staff are asked to relocate out into the branches for only a short period, with their long term career remaining at the organization's major centre.

In the second situation, the use of a two homes allowance may be less appropriate. Where there are multiple centres, each with career paths, employees may continue their careers within one place for some considerable time, with the need to move between centres reduced. To offer a two homes allowance under such circumstances may result in the individual not being fully committed to the new location, especially if the family remains behind in the old location.

Although the offer of two homes allowance may appear an attractive way of reducing resistance to relocation, there are a number of tax consequences which may make it less so. Briefly, there are capital gains tax implications from the ownership of two homes, income tax implications if the old home is rented out while the employee and family live in the new location and income tax implications for the relocation allowances package if the old home is not sold. Further details on the tax position are given in the next chapter.

As a result of this, two homes allowances for either the rent or purchase of a second property are an uncommon feature in relocation allowances policies. However, they are offered by a few large organizations, including BP and Unilever. At BP, existing employees may, under certain circumstances, elect to receive the company's 'rental option' as an alternative to a full house move. Under this scheme, the employee retains the old home when relocating to the new area and the company pays a contribution towards renting in the new area which varies according to the employee's marital status. It is normally paid in full for three years, after which payments are reduced. The scheme is taxable.

At Unilever, assistance given under the property retention scheme is based on the assumption that the employee lets the retained property and rents in the new area. The company normally pays the tax charges on the rental income, plus agents' fees. Employees also receive their disturbance allowance when they move, although this is taxable if they keep their old home. They also receive their transfer allowance (taxable) and one-off costs associated with the move. The property retention allowance (i.e. the tax on the rental income and agent's fees) tapers out over four years: it is paid in full for the first three years; is reduced by 50 per cent in year four and no allowance at all is paid in year five.

Company housing

Companies are not generally disposed towards owning houses, as this ties up large sums of capital which could be used more profitably in other ways. However, the provision of company housing can prove to be both an attractive benefit for employees and a means through which resistance to relocation can be overcome. Company housing is rarely provided long term, i.e. for several years at a time on relocation or indefinitely. It is more usual for it to be made available temporarily, for example to new employees who are relocated on recruitment and need some time to find and move into more permanent accommodation and for existing staff who need a temporary home in the new location because the dates of their job transfer and sale and purchase of property do not coincide. A survey from Alan Jones and Associates,[1] found that nearly 90 per cent of the survey participants provided no company accommodation at all, while just over 10 per cent provided either rented, subsidized rented or rent free accommodation. Around half the companies specified a time limit on the occupation of this accommodation: the average limit specified was 2.9 months for existing staff and 4.1 months for recruits. In general the accommodation was only available to managers or new graduates.

Equity sharing

When an employee is asked to relocate from a low cost to a high cost area, the house price difference may be so great that the gap becomes unbridgable and, because of seniority, lifestyle or family circumstances, the employee may be unwilling (or unable) to trade down to a more affordable property. The employee may still expect to be compensated for the difference in property prices for a move from like to like housing, while the employer finds the cost of the additional housing cost allowance – let alone any grossing up for tax and payment of National Insurance – to be prohibitively expensive. One solution may lie in equity sharing.

Equity sharing is a simple concept. It means that two or more people join together and combine their resources to buy a property. When employers are involved, the equity sharing arrangement is, at its simplest, between the employer and the employee, however, another party is usually involved – namely the employee's spouse.

There are two main advantages in using equity sharing. The employee could not afford to move without the financial input from the employer and so equity sharing provides a means of breaking down one of the barriers to relocation. Secondly, if property prices rise, the employer may recoup part of or all the cost of relocating the employee from the gain on sale when the property is eventually sold. The employer may even gain money from the arrangement when the sale is completed. Equity sharing is also extremely tax effective.

The disadvantages of equity sharing are numerous however. The main problem that employers face as soon as the property is purchased, is that of home improvements. All employees want to alter their homes to their own personal satisfaction and many home improvements affect the value of the property. The employer and employee must agree on how improvements are to be valued when the property is sold and employees should need the consent of their employer before carrying out any alterations. A statement to this effect should be incorporated into the legal agreement drawn up for the equity sharing arrangement.

There are a number of practical problems which can arise from the employee's personal circumstances. The legal documentation should spell out the need for the property to be sold, for instance, in the case of divorce. The spouse should be advised by his/her own independent solicitor and sign the equity sharing documentation to this effect.

When employees retire, it is standard practice under equity sharing documentation for the house to be sold and the employer to regain the appropriate level of equity and equity growth. Employees should be counselled and advised before signing an equity sharing agreement so that they realize the consequences of retirement upon their family's home.

The legal documentation should also spell out the company's line on recouping its money if the employee dies, is incapacitated permanently due to injury, leaves the company or wishes to change to another house.

Equity sharing documentation may provide for the employee to buy out (all or in part) the employer's share. If property prices increase rapidly, the employee is likely to find this difficult. Young employees are particularly badly hit as they are effectively unable to afford to trade up to bigger properties.

For the employer, maintaining adequate insurance cover on the property may prove to be a problem. The employer has an interest in the property and so wishes it to be fully insured; the employee, however, may not wish to insure the property or may forget to renew the cover. The employer could pay the whole insurance and deduct the appropriate sum from the employee's pay but in such a case the employee may complain about the cost, claiming that cheaper policies are available.

Equity sharing is certainly an area where disputes are likely. However, providing that proper legal documentation is drawn up before the parties enter into the equity sharing arrangement, the potential for conflict is reduced. Counselling employees on the effects that equity sharing has on their lives should also help to reduce the likelihood of problems and disputes.

A solicitor with expertise in this complex area is essential, not only to ensure that all legalities are tied up but also to reduce delay in the house buying process. A solicitor experienced in this field can draw up the necessary papers in a matter of days. In most equity sharing arrangements it is usual for a third party (a bank or building society) to lend some of the finance. However, standard bank home loan documentation is unsuitable for an equity sharing arrangement, because under this both the employer and the employee would be guaranteeing payment of the mortgage repayments. It is unlikely that the employer would wish to act as a guarantor for the employee's share of the mortgage. It is, therefore, necessary to ensure that special documentation is drawn up.

Delays in enacting the equity sharing arrangement can result in employees losing the property of their choice as another buyer with speedier access to funds steps in. It is important, therefore, that procedures to borrow funds from the bank are set up in advance, before any equity sharing arrangement is required.

There are now several hundred equity sharing cases operating in the UK but all are confidential. Employers keep such schemes just for one or two key individuals and secrecy is the norm.

Loans and mortgages

If house prices throughout the country were similar, employees could borrow sufficient funds through normal mortgage arrangements to buy their new properties. However, some staff face a gap in house prices which cannot be bridged through conventional means; additional housing cost allowances do not provide enough funding; and their employers do not wish to tie up company funds in houses through equity sharing. Other mortgage and loan arrangements, some directly through employers, others via third parties, have come into being to help solve these problems.

Company provision

Companies may offer some form of loan arrangement to assist employees moving into a high cost area, either in place of or in addition to an additional housing cost allowance. Loans may be interest-free or at low interest rates. Alternatively companies may use a variety of arrangements such as equity loans and deferred interest loans.

Low interest loans are most widely used in the finance sector. For example, in a recent survey conducted by Industrial Relations Services,[2] such loan schemes were available to employees in all the finance sector organizations surveyed, only occasionally being offered by those in other industry groups.

At Barclays Bank, for example, assistance is in the form of more generous terms under the staff house purchase scheme. Employees whose new workplace is within 36 miles of central London are able to borrow 4.5 times the main family salary including location allowance, or 3.5 times both partners' salaries and allowances with 5 per cent interest paid on the first £70,000 and bank rate thereafter. For employees whose new workplace is 36 to 55 miles from central London or within the South-East boundary, whichever is further, and staff moving to Edinburgh, Aberdeen, the Channel Islands and Isle of Man may borrow at 5 per cent interest on the first £60,000 using the same salary multipliers. For all other areas, the loan attracts interest at 5 per cent on the first £50,000, again with the same salary multipliers. The scheme is partially tax-free.

At the Midland Bank, staff are eligible for assistance if the differential in the bank's 'regional factor' between the old and the new areas is at least 20 per cent. The bank provides tax-free mortgage interest assistance, payable over four years with a maximum of £1,000 paid in the first year. A partially tax-free preferential rate loan scheme also applies. This has a limit of £50,000 with interest at 5.5 per cent. Salary multipliers vary according to the regional factor under the Midland's staff house purchase scheme.

At Nationwide Anglia, employees moving their workplace and home to within the Greater London and Outer Metropolitan areas receive tax-free excess rent allowances plus and additional £10,000 loan under the staff house purchase scheme. The normal loan is £30,000 at 4 per cent interest but for moves into the area noted above, an additional £10,000 may be borrowed at 6 per cent interest. This scheme is taxable.

Outside the finance sector, loan schemes are less common. However, in the Industrial Relations Services survey, a couple of schemes are highlighted. For example, Gallaher and Pilkington both offer loans to staff moving into high cost areas. At Pilkington, employees moving into higher cost areas outside London receive a loan at 1 per cent interest based on the house price differential to a maximum of £5,000 or 15 per cent of the purchase price to £5,000 maximum for first time buyers. Employees moving from outside London to within 20 miles of Charing Cross receive an interest-free loan of one-third of the price of the house up to 1.5 times salary. Both loans are taxable.

Although the provision of cheap loans is likely to remain a perk of the finance sector, with more generous terms offered on relocation into high priced areas, organizations in other industry groups are increasingly offering this benefit to relocated staff. According to Alan Jones & Associates' Relocation Policy Survey

Report,[1] of the 253 companies surveyed on this issue, two thirds provided company loans, although in many cases loans were discretionary or only paid in exceptional circumstances, to cover emergencies or only given to very senior staff.

The CBI Employee Relocation Council's research into relocation allowances[3] found a few organizations outside the finance sector with loan schemes. These included Du Pont, the Post Office and the United Kingdom Atomic Energy Authority. These organizations also operated additional housing cost allowance schemes.

In an attempt to help staff who are required to move from low to high cost areas The Boots Company plc has introduced a new loan scheme which is to be operated by Barclays Bank. Staff qualifying for a loan are first required to obtain a mortgage from their own building society or bank. This should be the maximum available (usually two and a half times appointment salary), although this limit may be reduced according to individual circumstances. Boots requires that employees invest all the equity from the sale of the existing house in the new property.

A loan is then made available to cover the difference between the mortgage and the amount required to purchase the property and is repayable in one amount after seven years. It may, however, be repaid earlier if the borrower wishes. Alternatively, it may be possible to continue the loan with Barclays, subject to mutual agreement between the borrower and the bank. The loan is also repayable in full immediately the borrower sells the property or ceases for any reason to be employed by any company controlled by Boots.

Barclays charges the employee interest on the loan at $1\frac{1}{8}$ per cent per annum above the bank's base rate, which approximates to an average mortage interest rate. There are no other charges associated with this loan.

Boots, however, subsidizes the interest payments on this Barclays loan in accordance with Table 4.

Although Boots pays a proportion of the interest for the first six years, there is no requirement for the employee to pay back any of that subsidized interest at any time in the future. Boots does not have any equity share in the property. The loan is unsecured.

The scheme has Inland Revenue approval and under current legislation the interest payments made by Boots are not taxed as a benefit-in-kind, unless or until they exceed a predetermined limit (this is £24,150 at the moment). This figure can be varied by the

Table 4
Boots/Barclays loan scheme

Year	% of interest paid by Boots	% of interest paid by employee
1	100	–
2	100	–
3	80	20
4	60	40
5	40	60
6	20	80
7	–	100

Inland Revenue from time to time. However, under current practice the limit in operation at the date on which a loan is secured remains valid for the whole of that loan period, irrespective of changes which may occur to the published figure.

If the company's interest payments during the seven year period exceed the Inland Revenue limit, benefit-in-kind tax only becomes payable by Boots above that limit value.

Company provided equity loans and deferred interest loans are uncommon. However, some of the building societies, such as National and Provincial, offer deferred interest loans to their staff on relocation in addition to their normal staff mortgages as a means of bridging large house price divides. Tax implications could, however, render such schemes financially unattractive to employees and, therefore, it is essential to obtain approval from the Inland Revenue before starting.

Third party arrangements
Third party arrangements include equity mortgage/equity financing/profit sharing loan schemes, deferred interest loans and shared ownership arrangements. In all but the last of these, under the various third party finance schemes, the employee and spouse own the property – not the company and not the third party.

Equity mortgages
Although somewhat limited in their availability, third party equity mortgages may provide a way to bridge the house price divide.

Put simply, these schemes provide low cost finance and/or the ability to borrow more than under a conventional mortgage, in exchange for a proportion of the equity growth on sale of the property. Such equity mortgages may also include an element of deferred interest.

Equity mortgages are rare, however, because lenders wish to ensure that equity growth is inevitable before launching such a product. It is unlikely that any employees would receive an equity mortgage if they move into an area of slow house price growth. Also, few lenders provide specifically targetted products to small selected areas of the market and relocated staff facing a huge mortgage increase only make up a small proportion of the mortgage market.

One of the few equity mortgage schemes available is that offered by Kleinwort Benson. Its 'Equity Mortgage Plan' has been developed to allow organizations the opportunity of providing an equity mortgage facility for their relocating employees without getting directly involved with the mortgage market or house ownership themselves. The plan is, however, only available to substantial companies and similar organizations and is not available to either the general public or small private concerns.

The Equity Mortgage Plan is designed to allow relocating employees the opportunity to borrow more than they would normally be able to do, but to have their monthly repayments geared directly to their ability to pay. Under the plan, the employee borrows three times salary (maximum) from Kleinwort Benson at its own mortgage interest rate as a principal mortgage. This is administered as a normal mortgage, with monthly interest payments and with a repayment term of 25 to 35 years (or age 70, whichever is sooner). The difference between the total of this mortgage plus the employee's equity and the purchase price is provided as an equity mortgage at 1 per cent over the normal mortgage interest rate. The amount loaned under the equity mortgage must not exceed 30 per cent of the total purchase price or valuation, whichever is the lower, and is covered by level term assurance. The total of the principal mortgage plus the equity mortgage does not exceed 80 per cent of the total purchase price or valuation, whichever is the lower.

The equity mortgage does not have to be repaid in monthly instalments. Interest is compounded at 1 per cent over the Kleinwort Benson mortgage rate and is repaid out of the property sale proceeds or by the employee buying out the equity mortgage.

The individual is required, however, to reduce the amount of the equity mortgage during the mortgage term by increasing the principal mortgage according to annual increases in salary after three years. Kleinwort Benson makes two charges in addition. A facility fee is charged to the company and there is an additional administration fee of 1.5 per cent of the outstanding balance of the equity mortgage when the property is sold or in any event after five years, assuming that the sum of the loan does not exceed the value of the property at that time.

Another equity mortgage scheme was that operated by the Nationwide Anglia Building Society in 1988 and 1989 for National Health Service employees working in the old GLC area of London. Nationwide Anglia Building Society has recently had to withdraw its 'Partnership Mortgage' scheme, largely because of its popularity. Although not linked to relocation, the principles of this low cost equity mortgage scheme are relevant to the subject.

Under the partnership mortgage, NHS employees borrow 4.5 times income (sole purchaser) or 3.5 times combined incomes or 4.5 times the main income plus 1.5 times the second income, to a maximum of £100,000, with interest paid at two-thirds of the normal rate for the whole life of the loan. In return, on sale of the property, the building society takes 50 per cent of the profit made by the borrower on the original portion of the property financed by the partnership mortgage. The profit calculation is based on the actual value of the property at the date of sale with the building society paying the cost of an independent valuation.

If the value of the property does not increase at a rate sufficient to provide the building society with a profit share large enough to cover the reduced interest rate charged, the borrower does not have to make up the difference. The building society's share of the profit is capped in two ways: the increase in value resulting from home improvements carried out by the borrower is ignored in the valuation on sale and, if the value of the property increases at more than 15 per cent per year throughout the life of the loan, the borrower keeps the excess in full. There is no time limit on when borrowers have to sell but the building society's share can be bought out by the borrower at any time and must be bought out when the balance outstanding on the loan falls below £5,000. A special life assurance policy operates, with the amount of cover increasing each year to ensure that both the loan and the building society's share is fully covered.

Since the launch of the NHS scheme, the Nationwide Anglia

Building Society has received many inquiries from other organizations, including a wide range of companies which have asked for
partnership mortgages to be made available to their staff being
relocated into the South East. It will be some time before the
scheme is extended. There are two main reasons for this. The
building society notes that cash flow is reduced during the life of
the loans and this will only be rectified when sales start to occur –
so build up of business must be gradual. Secondly, the Building
Societies Commission has set a 15 per cent Capital Adequacy
requirement for the loans, a figure equivalent to shared ownership.
(Capital Adequacy is the level of building society reserves which
must be set aside for each activity undertaken, against the
possibility of losses occurring. For comparison, the level is 4 per
cent for conventional mortgages.)

Deferred interest loans
Deferred interest loans involve payment of no interest or low
amounts of interest in the early years of the arrangement with
interest payments being 'rolled up' and repaid at the end or
towards the end of the life of the loan. Some of the interest charges
may be repaid out of the equity/equity growth. Commercial lenders
are generally not keen to offer such financing over a lengthy
period, for example over the 25 year life span of a conventional
mortgage, but may be willing to do so over a shorter period, say
five years. Deferred interest loans may, therefore, prove suitable
for employees who wish to retain their old home and buy a new
home in the new location with the expectation of selling it and
returning to the original base within a few years. However, with
regard to the tax treatment of deferred interest loans, difficulties
can occur over tax relief. Details are given in Chapter 4.

Shared ownership

When moving, most employees would like to buy their own house
or stay in owner-occupation. However, the price of housing in the
new area may prevent this. Shared ownership – through housing
associations – may provide a solution to the problem.

There are over 2,000 housing associations in the UK which are
registered with the Government's regulatory body, the Housing
Corporation. They are funded jointly by the Housing Corporation
and by local government, although private finance is increasingly

being used as well. Housing associations can acquire freeholds of land to build for shared ownership and can, in certain limited circumstances, also acquire existing property to provide shared ownership homes. (With shared ownership, existing units can normally only be purchased if the association is operating a Do-It-Yourself Shared Ownership (DIYSO) scheme. There is no grant funding available from the Housing Corporation for DIYSO schemes. A few local authorities do, however, make grant money available or even, in a limited number of cases, offer DIYSO facilities direct. Usually, however, the DIYSO schemes that do operate are aimed at existing council tenants or people on their housing waiting lists.)

Shared ownership provides 'half owned, half rented' accommodation and this is more easily affordable by employees. Employers who put up land or finance receive allocation rights in return, enabling them to offer lower cost housing to their employees than traditional owner-occupation. Under shared ownership schemes, employees can buy further shares in the property when able to do so. Depending on the scheme, the employer could gain an equity share in the ownership of the property. In a typical example £60,000 is required for a starter home. The employee might be able to afford to pay half this figure, using a combination of mortgage and equity. Of the extra £30,000, the housing association might borrow, say, £13,000 on a building society loan (special arrangements are available from building societies to provide low start loans, etc to housing associations). The employee would pay a monthly rent on this. The remaining finance could be provided by the Government in the form of a housing association grant, although this is not common in areas of rapid employment growth. So it is likely that the employer and/or the housing association would have to meet this shortfall. The provision of land by the employer for which planning permission could be obtained could help to reduce or even eliminate the need for the company to pay cash.

Besides providing homes on a shared ownership basis, housing associations can offer properties for rent at market rates under assured tenancies.

Rented accommodation

There are two schemes – the National Mobility Scheme and the Tenants Exchange Scheme – which operate through the National Mobility Office to help employees in certain types of rented accommodation to move into other areas. Although not a measure to overcome price differential barriers to moving, these schemes do provide a means by which council house and housing association tenants can move for employment reasons.

Under the National Mobility Scheme some 7,000 mobility cases are dealt with each year and of these around three-quarters concern rehousing for social reasons. The rest are for employment reasons. The majority of the cases concern council tenants, although the scheme also covers new town tenants, private tenants on waiting lists, housing association tenants and owner occupiers. Rehousing is, in the main, into council tenancies, although some people are rehoused into housing association or new town accommodation.

Local authorities are required to assist people with housing needs in their area. Although authorities try to help some people through key worker schemes, where employers approach the authority directly when moving staff, the numbers housed through such schemes are small. As a result, the National Mobility Scheme has operated since the early 1980s to handle housing needs arising through mobility. Almost all the local authorities and new towns in England, Scotland and Wales have joined the scheme and the Northern Ireland Housing Executive also takes part. Housing associations normally participate through the local authorities in which their properties are based and some of the larger housing associations participate directly in the scheme.

The National Mobility Scheme produces a pool of lettings and mobility cases. Those eligible to move are tenants of participating local authorities, new towns and housing associations, people high on housing waiting lists and others with pressing needs to move. They need to have sound employment or social reasons to move to somewhere beyond reasonable daily travelling distance from their present home.

A participating organization agrees to allocate at least 1 per cent of its estimated net lettings for incoming nominees, together with one letting for each of its own nominees rehoused elsewhere through the scheme. Net lettings include housing associations' lettings avilable to local authorities under nomination agreements. The participating organization agrees to work within the spirit of the scheme but has absolute discretion as to whether to make a nomination and whether to accept or reject a nomination received from another authority. Between them, the participating organizations are responsible for over 5 million public sector properties.

People interested in using the scheme do so by approaching the housing department of the local authority, new town, housing association or housing executive for the area in which they are presently living. If there appears to be reasonable prospects of a move, the housing authority makes a nomination to the authority to which the nominee needs to move. The organization which receives the nomination decides whether or not it can rehouse the nominee and, if it cannot, whether there is a housing association or new town in its area which might be able to assist.

Under the Tenants Exchange Scheme, public sector tenants are able to find partners with whom they might be able to exchange homes. Registrations are accepted from tenants of local authorities, new towns, housing associations and the Northern Ireland Housing Executive. Private tenants cannot use the list. Tenants wishing to exchange complete a registration form which is processed within two days and a letter confirming the registration details is sent to the tenant. Each month (except January) all local authorities and new towns are sent copies of the up to date computerized list of people wishing to move into that area. These lists are displayed to the public usually in housing departments and occasionally in libraries. Every six months tenants are asked to confirm that they are still looking for an exchange and, if not, their details are removed from the list.

Tenants use the list to find someone with whom to exchange homes. It is up to them to contact each other and arrange the exchange. They need their landlords' written consent to the exchange, but secure tenants in England and Wales have a statutory right to exchange homes which can only be refused on certain prescribed grounds. There is similar legislation in Scotland and Northern Ireland. The scheme is free to participants.

References

1 ALAN JONES & ASSOCIATES. *Relocation policy survey report*. Monmouth, Alan Jones & Associates, January 1989.
2 INDUSTRIAL RELATIONS REVIEW AND REPORT. 'Relocation survey 2: high

cost moves'. *Industrial Relations Review and Report*. No. 433, February 1989. pp 6–10.

3 CBI EMPLOYEE RELOCATION COUNCIL. *Survey of domestic and international relocation policies*. London, CBI Employee Relocation Council, February 1989.

Tax treatment of relocation allowances

Relocation has tax implications for employees and employers. Employees may be subject to income tax, National Insurance and capital gains tax. The taxation of relocation expenses is covered by two Extra-Statutory Concessions. This chapter explains what these concessions mean in practice and what employers can pay their employees tax-free. The tax implications of the various options to overcome the North-South divide are also explained. Relocation expenses affect employers' liability to corporation tax, National Insurance and VAT: this chapter also outlines employers' liabilities and the effects of relocation payments on company administration.

Taxes on individuals: Income tax

There is no statute law specifically governing the tax treatment of relocation expenses. As a result, *prima facie*, all relocation expenses paid by employers to employees earning £8,500 a year or more and to directors are subject to income tax. However, there are two Extra-Statutory Concessions relating to relocation – A5 and A67 – which allow for tax-free treatment provided that certain conditions are met. Guidance on the application of these Extra-Statutory Concessions is issued by the Inland Revenue to local tax inspectors. This is based on the tax treatment of relocation policies operating within the Civil Service. In other words, the tax treatment of relocation expenses paid to relocating Civil Servants (including tax inspectors, amongst others) is generally viewed by the Inland Revenue as being the benchmark against which the reasonableness of employers' relocation policies – and hence their request for favourable tax treatment – are judged. It is important to remember that although individual tax inspectors follow Inland Revenue Head Office guidance individual cases can be treated differently, according to circumstances.

In Chapter 2, the relocation allowances package is broken down and analysed under six main categories all of which have income tax implications for employees:

- direct costs
- indirect costs
- costs incurred when purchases and sales do not coincide
- commuting, househunting and moving expenses
- loss of income
- increased cost of accommodation.

Direct costs

Extra-Statutory Concession A5 states: 'In practice no assessment is made in respect of removal expenses borne by the employer where the employee has to change his residence in order to take up a new employment, or as a result of a transfer to another post within an employer's organisation, provided that the expenses are reasonable in amount and their payment is properly controlled.' (The full text of Extra-Statutory Concession A5 is given in Table 5.)

Table 5
Extra-Statutory Concession A5

A5   Expenses allowances and benefits in kind.

(a) Removal expenses
Under Chapter II Part V Income and Corporation Taxes Act (ICTA) 1988 expenses allowances and benefits in kind received by directors and by senior employees are assessable to tax as emoluments of the director or employee subject to a deduction for expenses incurred which satisfy the conditions laid down in Section 198, ICTA 1988. In practice no assessment is made in respect of removal expenses borne by the employer where the employee has to change his residence in order to take up a new employment, or as a result of a transfer to another post within an employer's organisation, provided that the expenses are reasonable in amount and their payment is properly controlled.

'Removal expenses' includes such related items as a temporary subsistence allowance while the employee is looking for accommodation at the new station. It also includes the reimbursement of interest payable on a bridging loan, provided it is confined to the net interest after tax relief, and the benefit from a 'cheap' or interest-free bridging loan in excess of £30,000 which would otherwise be chargeable to tax under Chapter II, Part V, ICTA 1988. A bridging loan will qualify for this treatment if all the following additional conditions are satisfied:

● The loan does not exceed a reasonable estimate of the market value of the old property. If the loan does exceed this amount the excess will not be regarded as a bridging loan for the purpose of this paragraph. Any such excess may, however, qualify for the treatment described in paragraph (b) below if the conditions described in that paragraph are fulfilled.

● The loan must be used only to bridge an unavoidable gap between the date expenditure is incurred on the purchase of the new property and the date on which the sale proceeds of the old property are received.

● The loan must be used only to pay off the mortgage on the old property, to fund the purchase of a new property or to meet immediately related incidental expenditure (eg legal or survey fees).

● Where the employer reimburses the bridging loan interest, that interest must be payable by the employee within 12 months from the making of the loan; in the case of the benefit of a 'cheap' or interest-free bridging loan, that loan must be outstanding for no more than 12 months (or in each case such longer period as the Board may allow).

(b) 'Cheap' or interest-free loans
Where a director or an employee who is paid at the rate of £8,500 a year or more has both a bridging loan eligible for relief under the concessionary treatment outlined above and a 'cheap' or interest-free loan, the benefit of which is chargeable under Section 160, ICTA 1988 (loans obtained by reason of employment), both loans are taken into account for the purpose of calculating any relief due under Part III, Schedule 7, ICTA 1988 against the charge under Section 160. In practice no charge will be made under the provisions of Chapter II, Part V, ICTA 1988 in respect of such part of the benefit of a 'cheap' or interest-free loan which is chargeable only because of the existence of a bridging loan which satisfies all the conditions set out in paragraph (a) above.

(c) Overseas duties – precarious health
Where a director or an employee who is paid at the rate of £8,500 a year or more goes abroad on a business journey and,

> although fit to carry out his duties at his normal place of work, takes his wife with him because his health is so precarious that he cannot undertake foreign travel unaccompanied, no charge is made under the provisions of Chapter II, Part V, ICTA 1988 in respect of expenses of the wife which may be borne by the employer.

Crown copyright.
Reproduced with the permission of the Controller of Her Majesty's Stationery Office.

The following points are crucial if tax-free treatment is to be obtained:

- The expenditure must be borne by the employer.
- The expenditure must be reasonable in amount and must be properly controlled. A written policy assists in proving proper control. Amounts broadly in line with Civil Service practice are likely to be considered reasonable.
- Employees must change their residence. This means selling the old home or giving up rented accommodation in the old location in order to purchase or rent a new property in the new location. First-time buyers are eligible for tax-free treatment.
- There are no laid down rules on eligibility with regard to distance or travelling time. However, it is expected that any relocation will significantly reduce an employee's travel to work journey either in distance or in time.

Who is covered?
Both new recruits and existing staff who are transferred are eligible for tax-free treatment.

What is covered?
Extra-Statutory Concession A5 does not provide a list of items considered by the Inland Revenue to be 'direct' relocation expenses. However, a suggested – but not exhaustive – list is reproduced in Table 6. Employers are advised to reach agreement with their local tax inspectors, in writing, on the direct expenses of relocation which may be paid tax-free to employees. Employers should remember that the concessional nature of the tax treatment leaves inspectors with a degree of discretion over whether the expenses claimed are allowable; employers can therefore negotiate items to be included as tax-free and the levels of amount considered

reasonable, although these are likely to be no more than reimbursement of costs incurred.

Table 6
Direct expenses of removal

1 The normal expenses of transporting household furniture and effects (including ordinary gardening equipment) belonging to the employee, his family and other dependants of his at the time of the move. Included are the costs of moving ordinary domestic pets but not other livestock or any exceptional possessions.

2 Temporary storage charges where furniture and effects cannot be moved directly to the new home.

3 The cost of travel between the old and new homes for the employee, his family and other dependants. Reasonable subsistence may also be paid where the length of the journey merits it.

4 The normal fees of solicitors and estate agents for house purchase and sale (and the equivalent where property is leased).

5 Stamp duty.

6 Land registration fees.

7 Normal expenses connected with a mortgage or loan, including mortgage guarantee and survey fees (but not interest).

8 Private survey fees including the cost of additional tests of the electrical wiring, heating installation and drains.

9 National House Building Council inspection fees, certificate charge and the premium for top up cover against inflation.

10 Insurance of household furniture and effects while in transport or in store provided this is not covered by the employee's existing insurances.

11 Abortive expenditure within any of the headings above provided that either:
   - the transaction did not proceed for reasons outside the employee's control;
   or
   - the employee's reasons for withdrawing were entirely reasonable in all the circumstances.

Indirect costs

Extra-Statutory Concession A5 also covers the tax treatment of the indirect costs incurred by employees on relocation and the same conditions as noted for direct costs apply. However, the payment of the disturbance allowance is one of the most controversial elements in the relocation package. The overriding principle regarding the tax-free treatment of disturbance allowances is that employees should not be better off as a result of tax-free payments on relocation than they were before the transfer.

Who is covered?
Both new recruits and existing staff who are transferred are eligible for tax-free treatment.

What is covered?
Extra-Statutory Concessions A5 does not provide a list of items considered by the Inland Revenue to be 'indirect' relocation expenses. However, as with direct costs, a suggested – but not exhaustive – list is reproduced in Table 7.

Table 7
Indirect expenses of removal

(Where appropriate, expenditure is subject to the betterment restriction at the end of the list.)
1 Taking down and re-fixing fixtures and fittings, including the cost of altering and adapting them for the new home.
2 Relaying floor coverings, including the cost of altering and adapting them for the new home.
3 Replacement curtains and floor coverings where the originals cannot be adapted for the new home.
4 The initial cleaning of the new home.
5 Disconnection and reconnection of domestic appliances, gas fires and fittings.
6 Replacement cooker where the original cannot be adapted to the fuel supply at the new home.
7 Reinstallation or replacement of a TV or radio aerial.
8 Installation of an ordinary domestic telephone provided the employee had one in his old home.
9 Any loss on domestic telephone rentals at the old location which cannot be recovered.
10 Any loss on an existing season ticket which cannot be

recovered.

11 Any irrecoverable part of a subscription to a club which can no longer be used. The initial cost of entering a comparable club but not the normal annual subscription.

12 Day school fees for the employee's children at the old location for the remainder of the term current at the time of removal but only where double payment for the same term is involved.

13 A contribution for up to two years towards the board and lodging costs of a child who attends a day school at the old location and who must be left behind when the family move in order to complete a course of study leading to an important examination.

A contribution may also be made where the child has to be sent to lodge at the new location in advance of the family move in order to start the course of study. The exemption ceases when the rest of the family move to the new location.

14 Where 13 above applies the employer may also reimburse tax-free reasonable expenses incurred by the child in travelling between the school and the family home:
 • at the beginning and end of term; and
 • on one other occasion during each term.

15 Travel and subsistence expenditure while searching for accommodation and while travelling temporarily before moving.

16 Interest on bridging loans (as now).

17 Actual loss on sale of old property.

Betterment restriction

(a) The tax-free payment must not do more than enable the employee to purchase assets of an equivalent quality, quantity, type, capacity, condition, etc, to those at the old home. The employer can pay more if he chooses but the tax-free element must be restricted accordingly.

(b) Claims must be restricted by the amount of any recovery from the disposal of old assets or if the old assets are retained, by their market value.

For example, an employee who has old and cheap carpet in a one bedroom flat at his old location cannot be paid tax-free the cost of new and expensive carpet for a five-bedroom house at his new location. He can only be paid tax-free the net cost of replacing an equivalent quantity of similar carpet in a similar condition.

Employers are advised to reach agreement with their local tax inspectors, in writing, on the indirect expenses of relocation which may be paid tax-free to employees, if they plan to pay each item separately. Alternatively, if employers prefer (for administrative simplicity) to pay a lump sum to cover indirect costs, the amount should be agreed with the tax inspector, in writing. Expenses must be 'reasonable in amount' and their payment 'must be properly controlled'. The amounts considered reasonable by the tax inspector are likely to be those paid in the Civil Service, although employers may negotiate for, and achieve, better treatment. The rates paid in the Civil Service vary from time to time. The Civil Service grants listed below took effect from 1 April 1988.

	Transfer grant
Single officer	£ 475
Married officer – no children	£1,580
Married officer – with children	£1,973

Single officers were also entitled to a miscellaneous expenses grant as follows:

	Miscellaneous expenses grant
Householder	£732
Non-householder (with more than one room)	£366
Non-householder (one room only)	£ 54

However, the Inland Revenue Head Office stated that tax inspectors would only apply a simplified two-tier structure of allowance to industry, depending on marital status, as follows:

Married staff – irrespective of whether the employee had children	£1,973
Single staff	£1,207*

*This figure was calculated by adding together the single officer's transfer grant of £475 and the householder's miscellaneous expenses grant of £732.

On 19 December 1989, HM Treasury announced a new transfer grant system for the Civil Service. Civil Service departments now have discretion to choose between a reimbursement system, where individuals are reimbursed additional expenditure supported by receipts (of the kind covered by the transfer grant and miscellaneous expenses grant) to an overall ceiling of £3,500 *or* a simplified – and more generous – flat rate system where the maximum levels of reimbursement are £2,200 for a married officer, £1,300 for a single householder and £500 for a single non-householder. Such payments are tax-free.

Employers may agree with their tax inspectors to reimburse actual disturbance expenses incurred by employees as shown by the production of receipts on a tax-free basis. The overall maximum figure of £3,500 is a Treasury imposed limit on Civil Service departments; it does not apply to employers. Hence, reimbursement for disturbance costs made by employers to employees may exceed this figure, provided that any such payments do not duplicate other amounts already paid, that receipts are produced, and that there is satisfactory evidence to show that the reimbursement of expenses does not exceed the necessary expenditure incurred by employees who have to move house with their jobs.

Alternatively, employers may follow the new, simplified, three-tier flat rate disturbance payment system. Provided that agreement is reached with local tax inspectors and that the inspectors are satisfied that payments given do not over-compensate employees (e.g. they are not being paid as an incentive to move), then there is no requirement for receipts to be produced and employers may pay the flat rate sums tax-free to their employees.

The effective date of these new arrangements is 19 December 1989.

Calculation of the disturbance allowance
As noted in Chapter 2 employers may base their disturbance payments on a percentage of salary; on a number of month(s) salary; grade, or on personal circumstances. Allowances may be given as flat-rate sums; two disturbance allowances may be given; or a disturbance allowance with additional payments for such items as school fees/uniforms given. The range of practice is diverse.

With regard to tax treatment, bearing in mind the likely overall tax-free maxima indicated above, employers may encounter the following:

• Tax inspectors may be concerned that disturbance allowances that are linked directly to pay may unfairly over-compensate employees for the upheaval of moving. Indeed, such payments may be viewed by tax inspectors as 'pay' and therefore be deemed to be fully taxable. Allowances related to employees' personal circumstances or less directly related to pay (eg related to grade, or paid as a flat-rate) are more likely to be considered as suitable recompense for the indirect costs of moving.

- If employers give two payments for disturbance, regardless of terminology (transfer grant, disturbance allowance, disturbance grant, relocation grant, etc) it is unlikely that both payments will attract tax-free treatment. One payment is likely to be tax-free (to the maximum level permitted by the tax inspector); the other, taxable.
- Additional items paid for by the employer, over and above the disturbance allowance, may prove to be tax-free in the employee's hands. As a result of negotiations with individual tax inspectors, some items may be allowed as a trade-off against other items in the package.

Costs incurred when purchases and sales do not coincide

These costs include:
- bridging loans
- guaranteed price schemes
- temporary accommodation.

Bridging loans
Extra-Statutory Concession A5 'also includes the reimbursement of interest payable on a bridging loan, provided it is confined to the net interest after tax relief, and the benefit from a "cheap" or interest-free bridging loan in excess of £30,000 which would otherwise be chargeable to tax under Chapter II, Part V, ICTA 1988'. Four additional conditions are attached – see text of Extra-Statutory Concession A5 in Table 5.

The following points are crucial to obtain tax-free treatment:

- The loan must not exceed a reasonable estimate of the market value of the old property but, if it does, providing the conditions set under section (b) of the Extra-Statutory Concession are met, the loan may still be tax-free. Employers are advised to obtain qualified independent fair market valuations of the property.

- Employees must not use the loan for any purpose other than paying off their old mortgage, buying their new property or paying related fees. In other words, employees cannot draw out funds from the loan (even their own equity) to buy other items such as a car or a holiday, otherwise the tax-free provision does not apply.
- The Extra-Statutory Concession states a limit of 12 months for tax-free treatment but it does contain the clause 'or in each case such longer period as the Board may allow'. In practice the Inland Revenue recognizes that employees may not be able to sell their properties within 12 months and it has been known for tax-free treatment to apply to loans outstanding for as long as three years. However, tax inspectors are likely to expect employees to take all reasonable steps to ensure the sale of the property such as maintaining it in a saleable condition.

Who is covered?
Both new recruits and existing staff who are transferred are eligible for tax-free treatment.

Guaranteed sale price schemes
Employers may operate guaranteed price schemes themselves or engage a third party specialist relocation management company (see Appendix 2). When a third party is used, employers pay a management fee to the third party. There is no benefit-in-kind liability on the employee as a result of the payment by the employer of this management fee.

The operation of guaranteed sale price schemes is described in Chapter 1 and company practice given in Chapter 2. In brief, employees receive a guaranteed price for their property and use this money to buy a new home, leaving the employer or the third party to dispose of the old one. In effect, the funds released to the employee from the old home are treated as bridging finance for tax purposes. Income tax implications may arise on the sale of the old home if it is eventually sold for more or for less than the guaranteed price given to the employee, if the employer passes on the profit or makes up any shortfall.

Third party relocation companies operate two main types of guaranteed sale price schemes: 'purchase sub-sale' and/or 'bridging finance'.

Under the purchase sub-sale arrangement, the relocation company exchanges contracts with the employee to buy the home.

Powers of attorney are used to create rights to hold, lend against, administer and finally sell on the home. Technical title remains vested in the owner, although beneficial interest passes to the relocation company. The completion is delayed until an incoming buyer is found, at which time the sale is completed and stamp duty is payable by the incoming purchaser.

If the property sells for less than the guaranteed price, the employee is not liable for income tax. This is because the 'event' for tax purposes is the exchange of contracts, provided that the contract is not conditional, between the employee and the relocation company.

Under the bridging finance system, a loan is created directly to the employee by the relocation company or by an outside source of finance. Powers of attorney are sometimes used but no exchange of contracts occurs. The bridging loan continues with the employer paying the interest until a buyer is found.

If the property sells for less than the bridging loan (i.e. the guaranteed sale price) and the employee receives a further sum from the employer to make up this loss on sale (i.e. the shortfall), it may be argued that this further payment is a benefit in kind and is, therefore, subject to income tax. However, different tax inspectors have issued different decisions on this issue. By making sure that the following points are complied with, it is likely that tax-free treatment will be obtained:

- The guaranteed price offered to the employee either by the employer or the third party must be based on a fair market value. This, in effect, means that any valuation must be carried out by qualified independent experts. It is advisable for two independent valuations to be taken, and an average calculated. If the valuations differ widely, for instance by more than 5 per cent, it is advisable for a third to be taken. An average of two or all three should then be calculated and used as the guaranteed price.
- Active steps must be taken to market the property and any such marketing must be controlled (i.e. not simply left to the employee).

The use of a guaranteed sale price scheme may have Capital Gains Tax implications (see page 104).

Who is covered?
Both new recruits and existing staff who are transferred are eligible for tax-free treatment.

The community charge (poll tax)
Employees on bridging loans or involved in guaranteed sale price schemes keep technical title to their old home after they have moved into their new one in the new location. Therefore, they are liable to pay the community charge in respect of the old home as a 'second home'.

For the first three months after a house has been vacated no community charge is liable. Thereafter, a local authority may set the standard charge on second homes at any one of five multiples betwen 0 and 2 of the personal community charge.

Payments by employers towards employees' community charge will not qualify for tax-free treatment under Extra-Statutory Concession A5.

Loss on sale
If a new or an existing employee is asked to relocate by a certain date and this results in the employee having to accept a 'forced sale' of his or her old property at below the market rate, employers may make up this loss on sale to the employee with no income tax charge arising from this payment. However, if tax-free treatment is to be achieved, it is crucial that the market value of the employee's old property is established by means of qualified independent valuations. As with the determination of the guaranteed price under a guaranteed price scheme, it is advisable to take valuations from two or three qualified, independent valuers before arriving at a fair market value for the property.

Loss on purchase price
Employees may find that, when they come to sell their properties as a result of a relocation, they are unable to achieve a selling price equal to the purchase price that they paid for the property. This may be because of a catastrophic collapse in house prices in their particular locality or because of a more general, depressed housing market. Employers may wish to make up any loss on purchase price but there may be income tax implications for both new and existing employees.

In the case of a huge local collapse in house prices, it is usual for tax inspectors to allow employers to make up any shortfall between the eventual sale price and the original purchase price on a tax-free basis. Agreement should be reached in writing, however, before any payments are made. No tax-free treatment is allowed for compensation for any hypothetical loss of equity growth: only compensation for true cash losses may be made tax-free.

If, however, the housing market is generally depressed, the case is less clear cut. Employers have a good business reason for relocating their employees at a particular time and cannot wait while employees sit tight and wait for house prices to rise. As a result, there is a case for payments for the loss on purchase price to be tax-free. However, if the housing market is generally depressed, employees are likely to save money on the purchase of their next property and so their loss on the purchase price of their old home is offset by the reduced price of their new home. In such circumstances, employers are advised to discuss the situation with their tax inspectors and achieve agreement in writing before making any payments to employees.

Temporary accommodation
Extra-Statutory Concession A5 states: ' "Removal expenses" includes such related items as a temporary subsistence allowance while the employee is looking for accommodation at the new station.' Again, any expenses borne by the employer must be 'reasonable in amount' and their payment must be 'properly controlled'. Employers should, therefore, obtain agreement from their local tax inspectors as to the level of daily/weekly allowance payable.

Who is covered?
Both new recruits and existing staff who are transferred are eligible for tax-free treatment. Employees' families may also live in temporary accommodation if the old home has been sold and the new property is temporarily unavailable for occupation.

If an employee's children have to remain in the old location while the family move to and live in the new location, temporary accommodation may be paid for by the employer on a tax-free basis for the children in the old location or for the employee/family in the new location.

What is covered?
In general, the employee's hotel or lodging costs, subsistence expenses, and weekend travel home costs are considered as allowable items for tax purposes. If the family is living in temporary

accommodation, hotel or lodging costs, subsistence expenses and occasional travel expenses to the old location to maintain the old property in a saleable condition are considered as allowable items for tax purposes. However, some tax inspectors may expect employers to deduct normal home living cost expenses from any payments made to the family living in temporary accommodation, because the family is no longer paying normal outgoings such as rent, rates, mortgage payments, etc. Practice amongst tax inspectors is diverse and employers are advised to negotiate on this and obtain agreement on allowable expenses in writing.

A point to note is that temporary accommodation and related expenses are generally only tax-free for 12 months. Employees may be asked to provide some proof of the fact that they are trying to find a permanent home in the new location, otherwise they may be considered to have two homes, which attracts certain tax penalties (see page 100).

Commuting, househunting and moving expenses

Commuting

As a general rule, all commuting expenses borne by employers are taxable in the employees' hands. However, if an employee (a recruit or an existing member of staff) is undecided as to whether to relocate or to commute to the new location, additional travel costs (ie the difference between the home and old work station, and home and the new work station) may be paid by the employer on a tax-free basis for up to a year.

Travelling expenses incurred through visiting the old home while living in temporary accommodation are considered tax-free under Extra-Statutory Concession A5 (see Temporary accommodation, on page 91).

Househunting and moving

Reasonable househunting and moving expenses for new and existing employees and their families may be paid tax-free. These include travel costs, as well as lodging and subsistence where the journey warrants it. These expenses are covered by Extra-Statutory Concession A5.

Loss of income
Employers may compensate employees for such items as loss of London weighting and/or loss of the spouse's income. Any such payments given are subject to income tax.

Increased cost of accommodation

Chapter 2 examines company practice with regard to paying an additional housing cost allowance to employees relocating into a more expensive housing area. Chapter 3 examines additional housing cost allowances along with other options to assist employees relocating into more expensive regions. These include the payment of a 'two homes' allowance; the provision of company housing; the use of equity sharing; provision of interest-free or low interest loans, equity loans and deferred interest loans; and the use of shared ownership. The following sections analyse the income tax implications of these options.

Additional housing cost allowances (AHCA)
For many years, an unpublished Inland Revenue Concession enabled employers to make payments to provide some level of compensation to existing staff transferred into high cost housing areas at company request. On 18 January 1985 this was officially issued as a Statement of Practice (SP1/85). Payments were limited to 'reasonable maxima' (in line with Civil Service payments) based on two scales: transfers to London and transfers elsewhere. Before 1 April 1987, Civil Servants could receive up to £7,966 (spread over nine years) on being moved to London, or up to £4,095 for moves between areas outside London.

As from 1 April 1987, the Civil Service scheme was made more sensitive to house price differentials, which meant that, under the new arrangements, some people would get more and some would get less than would have been the case under the old scheme. The absolute ceiling was raised to £18,270, payable over nine years.

On 28 October 1987, the Inland Revenue republished the Statement of Practice (SP1/85) as an Extra-Statutory Concession. This is now Extra-Statutory Concession A67. The full text of this is given in Table 8.

Table 8
Extra-Statutory Concession A67
Payments to employees moved to higher cost housing areas

Where employees or office holders are compulsorily transferred within an organization by their employer and, as a result, have to change their residence, they may have to move to an area where the cost of accommodation (whether rented or purchased) is higher than before. If the employer makes a contribution towards these extra costs, any such payment forms part of employees' income from their employment and is chargeable to income tax under Schedule E. Provided, however, such payments are clearly linked to the ongoing cost of accommodation at the new location and the following conditions are satisfied, they are regarded as non-taxable:

(a) The terms of the employer's scheme restrict payments by reference to the price or rent of accommodation in the new location roughly equivalent to that previously owned or rented. For example, allowances should not be payable in respect of the costs of a four-bedroomed detached house where a two-bedroomed terraced house was previously occupied.

(b) Payments are restricted to an amount which approximately represents the reimbursement of outgoings of a revenue nature, eg rent, rates, ground rent, mortgage interest, etc as distinct from items of a capital nature eg mortgage loan repayments, the cost of house extensions, etc.

(c) Any tax allowances claimable must be taken into account. An employee who receives reimbursement of, or a payment in respect of, additional mortgage interest payable, can generally claim some or all of that interest as a deduction for tax purposes. Any payment under the scheme is therefore treated as exempt only where it can be regarded as covering the net cost to the recipient.

(d) The payments must be for a limited period of time and must taper as the years progress.

(e) The payments must not be in the form of a lump sum payment made at the time of transfer.

(f) The total of payments made over the entire period is limited to the maximum amount payable in the Civil Service. If the amounts paid exceed the maximum amount payable in the Civil Service, but conditions (a) to (e) are met, the excess is taxed on a *pro rata* basis for each of the years concerned.

Crown copyright.
Reproduced with the permission of the Controller of Her Majesty's Stationery Office.

Who is covered?
Extra-Statutory Concession A67 only applies to relocated existing employees and not employees who move in order to take up a first job within an organization, i.e. employees must be 'compulsorily transferred'.

Calculation
The additional housing cost allowance (AHCA), as it is called in the Civil Service, is calculated by multiplying the difference between house prices of comparable housing in the old and new locations by the average mortgage interest rate after tax relief, multiplied by the total length of the taper. In the Civil Service, the maximum difference in house prices is £30,000; the Inland Revenue's current figure for the average mortgage interest rate after tax relief is 11.5 per cent; and the total length of the Civil Service taper is nine years. (Years one to five at 100 per cent, thereafter reducing by 20 per cent per year.)

The maximum tax free payments currently allowed under the Civil Service scheme are £3,450 per annum for five years (a total of £17,250); and then this figure is reduced to 80 per cent in year six (£2,760); 60 per cent in year seven (£2,070); 40 per cent in year eight (£1,380); and 20 per cent in year nine (£690). This gives a total of £24,150 tax-free over the life of the scheme.

These annual allowances are not applied as tax free maxima to industry – it is the overall maximum of £24,150 which is important for the purposes of satisfying the terms of the concession.

The amount payable tax-free varies as interest rates and income tax levels change. The most recent announcement came in the Inland Revenue's press release of 9 April 1990 and applies to moves which take place on or after 6 April 1990.

The Inland Revenue states that: 'The maximum aggregate and annual allowances have been as follows:

	Aggregate allowance £	**Annual allowance** £
1 April–30 May 1987	18,270	2,610
1 June 1987–29 March 1988	17,220	2,460
30 March 1988–30 September 1988	15,750	2,250
1 October 1988–31 January 1989	20,160	2,880
1 February 1989–30 November 1989	21,210	3,030
1 December 1989–5 April 1990	22,890	3,270
6 April 1990 onwards	24,150	3,450

'It is understood that provided the payments in any one year do not exceed the additional annual housing cost . . . it is considered acceptable for the payments to extend for any period between four and nine years if the aggregate allowance is not exceeded and the payments for the penultimate and final years represent in the region of two-thirds and one-third respectively of the amount paid in the ante-penultimate year. Thus, for instance, if the aggregate allowance is £20,160, as it was in late 1988, and additional annual housing costs of £7,560 can be justified in the first year, one could pay the balance of £12,600 over the next three years in annual amounts of £6,300, £4,200 and £2,100, provided in each year the payments can be justified by reference to the additional housing costs.'

Establishing house prices
House prices in the new and old locations must be established by using a reliable and reputable source. Building society house price indices, such as those published by the Halifax Building Society, Nationwide Anglia Building Society and the Woolwich Building Society are all suitable. Alternatively, employers may use information provided by local independent valuers or relocation management companies.

It is not advisable to take the employee's word on values of new and old property. If house price differences amount to less than £30,000 the actual difference must be used in the calculation of AHCA, not the full £30,000.

Value of house
If the price of an employee's house is out of line with properties for the area, there are rules in the Civil Service to deal with this. These may be used as guidelines by employers (see Table 9).

Table 9
Calculation of maximum additional mortgage

This table shows the calculation of maximum additional mortgage where: A selling price of old property is more than 25 per cent above or below the listed average price for properties of that type at the location; and B the listed average price for properties of that type at the new location is higher than at the old location.

---

1 The following procedure should be adopted:
   (a) the normal calculation will first be made (see page 95).

(b) the result of (a) will then be adjusted by adding or subtracting, as appropriate, the result of the following formula;

$$\frac{A-(B \pm 25\%)}{B} \times (C-B)$$

Where: A=selling price of old property
B=average price for that property type in old area
C=average price for that property type in new area
(See examples below.)

2 If the selling price is not known when AHCA is claimed for accommodation at the new location, the current estimated value of the property at the old location should be used in the computation; and that computation should be reassessed, and any necessary extra payment or recovery made, on the basis of the actual selling price when the property at the old location is sold.

3 'Redemption money' paid to redeem feu duty or ground burden at the time of sale on properties sold in Scotland should be deducted from the sale price.

Example (a):
Selling price of old property £72,000
Average price for property type in old area £50,000
Average price for same property type in new area £70,000
1   (a) Normal maximum additional mortgage for AHCA purposes:
£70,000−£50,000=£20,000
(b) $\frac{72,000-(50,000 + 25\%)}{50,000} \times (70,000-50,000)$
=£3,800
Maximum additional mortgage to be taken into account in calculating AHCA:
£20,000 + £3,800=£23,800

Example (b):
Selling price of old property £35,000
Same locations and property type as Example (a)
1   (a) Normal maximum=£20,000
(b) $\frac{35,000-(50,000-25\%)}{50,000} \times (70,000-50,000)$
= −£1,000
Maximum additional mortgage to be taken into account in calculating AHCA:
£20,000−£1,000=£19,000

Source: Inland Revenue Head Office.

Trading up
If an employee trades up to a better house, no AHCA is payable on the betterment. A tax-free payment only applies to the additional cost incurred through moving from like to like property; any additional sums paid to the employee to assist with trading up are taxable.

Additional payments
Provided the basic rules of the concession are followed, employers can pay more, eg by basing house price differentials on a £50,000 house price gap. However, as the terms of Extra-Statutory Concession A67 indicate, amounts which exceed the specific maximum (currently £22,890) are taxed on a pro-rata basis. Inspectors require payment of income tax year by year (for instance if the sums paid exceed the employees' total annual additional housing costs). Employers are advised to agree with their tax inspectors whether – and if so, when – tax will become payable.

In the Civil Service, housing cost supplements of up to £10,000 may be paid at the discretion of the employing department when AHCA gives insufficient help with increased mortgage costs on buying at the new location. However, any such payments are taxable, although the employing department may make an addition of one-third when calculating the supplement to allow for payment of tax at the current standard rate of 25 per cent. No further adjustment may be made where the supplement is subject to tax at 40 per cent. The basic supplement is not subject to National Insurance, but contributions are payable in respect of the one-third addition to help with payment of tax. No compensatory payments may be made in respect of any National Insurance payable.

Change of ownership status
Employees moving from rented to purchased or from purchased to rented property may qualify for a tax-free AHCA. The additional cost calculation should refer to the property at the old location. For employees moving from rented to purchased property, the cost of the new property should be 'translated' into a rental equivalent and then compared with the rent at the old property for the purpose of the calculation. For moves from purchased to rented property, vice versa applies.

Changes in interest rates
The maximum amount payable tax-free varies with the date of the employee's move. For example, employees moving on 30 March 1988 up to and including 30 September 1988 continue to receive up to, but no more than, £15,750 tax-free, even though interest rates have subsequently risen. Employees moving on or after 6 April 1990 will continue to receive up to £24,150 tax-free over the life of their tapering arrangement, even if interest rates should subsequently fall.

Employers may wish to raise or lower payments in line with rising or falling interest rates and give the resulting sums tax-free to employees. Under the terms of Extra-Statutory Concession A67 this is unlikely to be approved by tax inspectors. However, employers may negotiate on this issue and may win approval for a fluctuating payment scheme in line with interest rates, provided that the amounts payable are capable of going both up and down. Agreement should be reached, in writing, with tax inspectors.

The community charge (poll tax)
This is a tax on individuals, not on property. Payments by employers towards employees' community charge will not qualify for tax-free treatment under Extra-Statutory Concession A67. However, some items such as additional house insurance costs may be paid tax-free along with additional mortgage interest payments, up to the prescribed maximum sum allowable, depending on employees' circumstances.

Length of taper
The length of the taper may be as little as four years or as long as nine, according to the Inland Revenue's head office. However, decisions on tapering arrangements are in the hands of local tax inspectors. Tapers as short as two and three years have been agreed in practice, as have tapers of 10 to 12 years. It is advisable to reach agreement with tax inspectors, in writing.

Further moves
Uncertainty may arise if employees undertake further relocations (either to cheaper or dearer areas) during the life of the tapering arrangement. The following are suggested solutions. If the employee moves during the period of the taper to a third location where housing is more expensive than in the first location, but is less expensive than in the second, tax inspectors are likely to

concede that it is reasonable to look back at the price of the first house and compare that with the price of the third house and recalculate the allowance on that basis for the remainder of the taper. If the move to the third property occurs after the end of the taper, it is reasonable to compare the price of the second house with the third house and as the third house is cheaper, no additional housing cost allowance applies. However, this is a negotiable situation and employers are advised to gain agreement, in writing, with their tax inspectors.

If, on the other hand, the employee moves during the life of the taper to a third property which is more expensive than the second location (which in turn is more expensive than the first), the same principles of 'reasonableness' should apply. It is possible, however, that employers may wish to end the first additional housing cost allowance at the date of the second move and institute a fresh allowance for the full period of the taper, not just the remainder of the taper. Tax inspectors are likely to have different views on the reasonableness of this approach and again employers are advised to gain agreement, in writing, with them. If the move to the third property takes place after the end of the first tapering arrangement, it may be treated as a fresh move, and a new allowance can be calculated and paid for the full length of the taper.

If the employee's third house is in a less expensive area than the original housing in the first location, most employers would cease paying any additional housing cost allowance on the date of the second transfer. To pay any such allowance in such circumstances is highly likely to attract tax.

Two homes allowances
The payment of an allowance to enable an employee to buy or rent a second home without disposing of the original home has several tax implications. Extra-Statutory Concession A5 refers to '. . . where the employee has to change his residence in order to take up a new employment, or as a result of a transfer to another post within an employer's organisation . . .' and Extra-Statutory Concession A67 refers to 'where employees or office holders are compulsorily transferred within an organisation by their employer and, as a result, have to change their residence . . .'

The Inland Revenue regards changing residence as selling the old home or disposing of the old rented accommodation. As a result, if employees retain possession of the old property, the

terms and conditions of both Extra-Statutory Concession A5 and
Extra-Statutory Concession A67 do not apply to the relocation.
In other words, strictly speaking, all relocation payments, allow-
ances and benefits are subject to income tax.

Certain 'detached duty' expenses may be paid tax-free if the
employee is renting, rather than buying, the second property.
When employees are required temporarily to work away from
their normal place of work for a period of 12 months or less,
inspectors of taxes will generally agree that the rent may be borne
by the employer without creating a taxable benefit.

If the employee buys or rents a new home and rents out the old
home, the rental income achieved is subject to income tax,
although deductions may be made for items such as normal repairs,
maintenance, rates and any management expenses incurred
through engaging a letting and/or management agent.

If the employee buys a second home, there are Capital Gains
Tax implications (see page 104).

Company housing

If the employer provides accommodation for the employee, this is
regarded as a taxable benefit. If the property is rented and the
employer pays the rent on behalf of the employee, the amount of
rent paid is treated as a taxable benefit and the employee pays
income tax on it.

If the property is owned by the employer and is worth less than
£75,000, the tax charge is equal to the gross rateable value of the
property. If it is worth more than £75,000, the employee pays
income tax on the level of the gross rateable value, plus income
tax on a sum equal to interest at the official rate on the amount of
the difference between £75,000 and the market value of the
property.

Following the introduction of the community charge, domestic
rating lists will become increasingly outdated. The government
has already announced that in consequence it is reviewing the long
term basis of the tax charge on living accommodation with a view
to introducing new rules for the future.

Equity sharing

Under an equity sharing arrangement, the tax charge is generally
a proportion of the gross rateable value equal to the proportion
of the total purchase price paid by the employer. If the employer's

share of the cost exceeds £75,000, there is an additional charge on a sum equal to interest at the official rate on the excess.

The equity sharing agreement can be structured so that either the employer or the employee can enjoy the gain on sale on the employer's share of the property. If the employer wishes to take some of the equity gain, the arrangement should be that of a proportionate purchase, with each party taking out equity growth in proportion to the amounts they both put in.

If the company wishes the employee to receive all the equity growth, it can operate the same proportionate purchase agreement but grant the employee an option at the time the property is bought to buy the employer's share for the original amount paid by the employer. Just before the property is sold, the employee exercises this option, acquires the employer's share for the original cost. The employee then owns the whole property, sells it and keeps the gain. The grant of an option gives rise to a tax charge on the difference between the consideration paid by the employee for that grant and the open market value of the option.

Alternatively, the agreement can be structured so that the employer takes out the original sum put in and the employee takes out all the rest, i.e. the employee's share, the gain on both the employee's and the employer's share. This arrangement will give rise to a tax charge, depending on exactly how it is structured.

Equity loans and deferred interest loans
Under equity loans and deferred interest loans from employers or third parties most, if not all, the interest due is deferred to a later date – when the property is sold or when the employee leaves the company. Some of the deferred interest payable depends on the increase in value of the property.

If the loan is made by the employer and interest is paid at less than the official rate, there is a taxable benefit (see interest-free or low interest loans below). However, when the deferred interest is paid, employees do not have the right to go back over the years of the loan and recalculate the taxable benefit taking into account the interest that has been paid. They can only go back for six years as the claims rules in Section 43, Taxes Management Act 1970 apply.

The employee qualifies for mortgage interest relief on the first £30,000 but interest relief is due on interest actually paid. Therefore, year by year, interest relief is only available for a small amount of interest, ie that which is actually paid each year. The

Inland Revenue does not allow deferred interest loans to be operated within MIRAS (Mortgage Interest Relief At Source). This means that the borrower may have to claim back the tax relief through the PAYE system.

Interest-free or low interest loans
Interest-free or low interest loans (which are not bridging loans under Extra-Statutory Concession A5) are regarded as beneficial loans and are subject to income tax. The tax charge is based on the difference between the official rate of interest and the interest charged by the employer to the employee. The first £30,000 of any such loan qualifies for tax relief provided that the employee is not already receiving relief on a loan from elsewhere.

Shared ownership
Under shared ownership arrangements employers put up money or land so that housing associations may build houses and in turn employers receive nomination rights to the properties. Under some schemes, employers keep an equity stake in the property. Employees pay a combination of mortgage and rent on the property. There is no income tax liability on employees under shared ownership schemes, provided the rent is a market rent.

National Insurance

Some relocation payments attract liability to National Insurance. These include the payment of round sum allowances as compensation for miscellaneous expenses incurred by employees and direct payments to employees.

Employees' National Insurance contributions are subject to an upper limit, currently £325 (contracted out rate), and so the majority of relocated employees will not see any increase in their part of the National Insurance contributions.

Benefits-in-kind and direct reimbursement of expenses incurred are not subject to National Insurance. 'Payments-in-kind' are also exempt. This means that if the employer uses a third party – a removal company or a relocation management company – so that services are provided to the employee and the employer pays the third party directly for these services, there is no National Insurance liability on the employee.

Capital Gains Tax (CGT)

A capital gain arises when an asset (such as a house) owned by an individual is given away, exchanged, sold or disposed of in any other way and its value has increased since the individual acquired it. Tax is not charged on the asset itself but on its gain in value. In general, only gains or losses (losses can usually be set against gains in the same tax year) since 31 March 1982 are taken into account and they are fully adjusted for the effects of inflation since that date. Individuals are allowed a certain amount of gains each year free of CGT (currently £5,000). As a general rule, individuals do not have to pay CGT if they own or co-own the property and it has been their only or main residence throughout the time they owned it; in other words, an exemption applies.

Individuals can only have exemption for one residence at a time, so if they own or co-own two homes they can choose which home is to be exempt and inform their tax office of this decision. If they do not do so, the determination will be made by the inspector of taxes.

When individuals acquire a further home, they normally have up to two years in which to inform their tax office of which one has been chosen to have the exemption as their main residence. Individuals can change their minds and nominate the other property for the exemption but this cannot affect the period more than two years before they make their new choice.

Married couples only have one exemption between them. Couples must choose which home has the exemption and both must tell their tax office of this decision.

Letting property also has CGT implications. If employees let part of their home to someone who is not treated as a member of the family, the gain on the part of the home which is let is exempt up to either the amount of exempt gain on the unlet part of the home or £20,000 which ever is the less.

If an individual owns two homes, absences from the main home may affect exemption. Providing the absence meets certain conditions, the individual may keep the exemption, see Table 10.

Table 10
Inland Revenue guidance on CGT

> **Q** Since buying my main home I have not lived there all the time. Do absences affect the exemption?

A Yes, except for the following:

    a Absences before 6 April 1965 (when CGT came into force) or 31 March 1982 (if the disposal was made after 5 April 1988),

    b Any absences during the two years before disposal,

    c Absence during the first year you own it when you do not move in immediately because

    either

    You are still living in your old home which you have not sold

    or

    You are having alterations made to your new home or having it redecorated,

    d An absence of any length after 31 July 1978 when you intend to live in your house, but for the present have to live elsewhere in a house provided by your employer so that you can do your job effectively,

    e An absence of any length after 6 April 1983 when you intend to live in your house, but for the present have to live in premises you do not own in order to carry on a business.

There are three further absences for which you may keep the exemption provided that:

- You live in the house as your main home at some stage both before and afterwards and
- There is no other house to which the exemption can be given during the absence.

These are:

    f Absences for whatever reason totalling not more than three years in all,

    g Absences during which you are in employment and all your duties are carried on outside the United Kingdom,

    h Absences totalling not more than four years when

    either

    The distance from your place of work prevents you living at home

    or

    Your employer requires you to work away from home in order to do your job effectively.

You will keep the exemption for absences under g and h if you cannot return home afterwards because your existing job requires you to work away again.

Where there are absences which affect the exemption, only part of the gain on the home is exempt. The amount exempt depends on when the disposal of your home takes place. If it was before 6 April 1988, the exempt amount is a proportion of the gain corresponding to the proportion of the period you owned the house for which exemption is due – but periods before 6 April 1965 are ignored for this. If it is after 5 April 1988, the rule is similar, except that periods before 31 March 1982 are ignored.

Example

31 March 1975	You bought your house and lived there.
31 March 1980	Your employer moved you to another part of the United Kingdom that was so far away you needed to stay in rented accommodation.
31 March 1988	You moved back into your own house.
31 March 1989	You sold the house.

Because you are selling your home after 5 April 1988 periods before 31 March 1982 can be disregarded.

Of the 6 years since 31 March 1982 you were away you are allowed 4 years under h and 2 years under f. This means that the whole period of 7 years since 31 March 1982 during which you owned the house will be exempt.

Source: Inland Revenue booklet CGT 4 Capital Gains Tax Owner-Occupied Houses.

The use of a guaranteed home sale scheme may also have CGT implications. Under 'purchase sub-sale' used by many third party relocation companies, a potential liability for CGT arises if any profit above the guaranteed price is paid to employees. Under 'bridging finance documentation', no liability exists because the 'event' for tax purposes is the price for which the property sells. The employee has only received a bridging loan to facilitate the new purchase.

Employer's liability

Corporation Tax
Relocation expenses of a revenue nature (for instance subsistence expenses, interest on bridging loans and direct relocation costs) which have been paid to employees may be offset as a business expense against Corporation Tax. No deduction is allowable for capital expenditure (e.g. house purchase).

National Insurance
There is no upper limit on employers' National Insurance contributions where these are applicable (see page 103).

Directors
Under the Companies Act, companies are prohibited from giving loans to directors. Directors are, therefore, unable to receive bridging loans from their own companies but companies may use guaranteed home sale schemes via third party relocation companies for directors. The administration of such schemes must be based on the principle of 'purchase sub-sale' and enable funding to come either directly from the relocation company or be provided by the employer as an off balance sheet item, not offending the Companies Act.

Making payment
The payment of round sum expenses must be administered via normal payroll procedures. They must not be paid directly to the employee thus leaving the onus on the employee to declare such income and expenditure on annual tax returns.

P11D dispensation
The two Extra-Statutory Concessions covering removal and relocation expenses allow tax-free payments to be made to employees, provided that certain circumstances are met. Nevertheless, employers are required to report these payments on employees' P11D forms, if they earn £8,500 a year or more. (P9D forms apply to those earning under £8,500 p.a.) If an organization intends to relocate several employees, it is administratively easier to obtain a P11D dispensation from the Inland Revenue and so remove the need for reporting requirements.

This is done by submitting a copy of the organization's relocation policy to the Inland Revenue, highlighting internal control procedures which are followed, the type and level of payments made and those for which tax-free payment is sought.

Value Added Tax (VAT)

VAT can normally only be recovered by a company when it relates to supplies bought for business purposes by the registered company and used by that company in making taxable goods, supplies and services.

Many relocation expenses fail these criteria and VAT is non-recoverable on them. For example, employers cannot reclaim VAT on expenses reimbursed by means of a flat rate allowance or round sum. VAT on payments for goods (as opposed to services) which remain the employee's property, not the employer's, are also not recoverable.

However, it is understood that HM Customs and Excise does permit the recovery of VAT (subject to normal input tax deduction) on the direct costs of relocation services such as estate agents' fees, solicitors' fees and removal contractors' charges, provided that the employer requires the employee to move house for business reasons, not personal reasons. Subsistence expenses (meals and accommodation) are allowable under paragraph 37 of The VAT Guide (HM Customs and Excise Notice 700), and paragraph 66 (e)(i) shows that an invoice made out to an employee will suffice. Otherwise it is advisable for employers to require invoices for relocation services expenses to be made out in the name of the company to claim recovery of the VAT as input tax.

Output tax should not be charged, as reimbursement of the cost of relocation services does not represent a taxable supply by the company to the employee. This is because the reimbursement of relocation expenses represents the reimbursement of business expenses incurred by employees in connection with their employment.

5

Group moves

This chapter examines why companies move, how moves are planned and implemented and the implications and practical effects on the workforces. Case studies are given of both long and short distance moves.

Why move?

Companies decide to relocate for a wide variety of reasons. These include:

- expiry of the lease on current premises
- high rent increases
- the opportunity to obtain freehold premises
- shortage of space and the need to accommodate growth/ expansion
- the start up and development of a new business
- the need to implement a new business strategy
- consolidation of existing business activities
- the need to integrate acquisitions
- to be closer to other operations in the case of mergers
- to improve access to services and/or customers
- to reduce high distribution costs
- the inability to attract staff
- difficulties in introducing new technology
- to improve or to create a new corporate image
- to reduce costs and/or obtain grants (see Appendix 1).

The relocation of a business is a costly exercise. It is, therefore, important to determine whether the problem which triggers the move can genuinely be solved by relocation. For example, relocating a business does not solve problems resulting from poor personnel policies, bad public relations, declining markets or reactive planning – to name but a few. A company's objective must be to resolve the business problem and, as such, relocation by itself or moving combined with other initiatives may not be the answer.

During 1988, Price Waterhouse in association with the CBI Employee Relocation Council carried out a survey[1] of just under 50 organizations to establish and understand the triggers which prompt relocation and the goals and selection criteria determined by companies on the move.

The survey found that poor accommodation and facilities were the main driving factors behind relocation. Typically, lack of space and increasing rents provided the major impetus. However, the survey found that very few organizations carried out audits of their accommodation or facilities on a regular basis to relate available space to future needs. As a result, many companies reacted late to increasing accommodation problems and were, therefore, driven into relocation after years of tolerating a worsening situation. The survey did find, however, that larger companies with directors or managers specifically responsible for facilities management functions did have a good perspective on long-term space needs.

The second most commonly quoted reason for relocation identified was the revision of business strategy and plans. This included relocation as a result of growth, new markets and new strategy. Costs were in third place and included accommodation, transport and staff costs. Changes in business structure, including mergers, acquisitions and rationalization, came fourth in order of importance and shortages of labour and skills were in fifth place. In general, the survey noted that companies are not usually forced to relocate as a result of labour or skills shortages: they are more likely to move because of the combined effects of problems, including shortages at their current locations.

Once the need to move has been identified, companies set objectives or goals for the relocation project. It would be expected that the goals would reflect the relative importance of the reasons established for moving. However, the survey did not show this to be the case. Financial aspects came to the fore, with the greatest importance attached to reducing costs. These included reducing rents, rates, salaries, transport and materials costs. Savings – for example through operations integration – were considered important, as were grants.

In second place in the list of goals, not surprisingly, emerged the need to acquire suitable accommodation – reflecting the most important trigger which prompted the relocation in the first place.

Other factors which were seen as equally important were the need to implement new technology, improve communications with customers and suppliers and to maintain or improve the human resource and skills base. The need to improve the company's image was also regarded as important but was not a major relocation goal by itself.

The survey found that some companies going out of London and the South East moved to areas with large and less expensive labour pools. They expected to recruit from other employers in the area, rather than from the unemployed labour force. It also found that companies relocating to the South East did so to be closer to customers in an area where economic activity is high. This was done in some cases by setting up a sales office in the South East rather than relocating the whole workforce.

Many organizations based in London move out to reduce rent and rates costs and to get benefit from better accommodation and transport rather than to reduce staff costs. Many firms moving out of the capital move short distances – less than 100 miles – so they can keep existing managerial staff, maintain continuity of operations and also retain links with the capital.

Reasons for moving and goals might be expected to form the basis of the selection criteria used to determine the new location. However, the survey found that companies' site selection decisions were based on the need to 'reduce the immediate trauma of relocation'. So, although access to communication networks was one of the most important factors in site selection, the quality of the environment and the ability to transfer staff and recruit available labour were seen as crucial to the success of the move. The size of premises and opportunities for expansion, as well as the image of the area, were also considered important. Financial incentives – such as grants – were not of major importance in site choice.

Goals did not match site selection criteria because, it seems, provided that the cost of the new location is reasonable, then maximum cost savings are not as important as good access to customers and suppliers and providing a location that is attractive to senior staff. The relocation must be low risk rather than low cost.

Culture

Developing a mobility culture
Organizations rarely change their location regularly. A group move exercise is likely to take place only once, if at all, in an employee's working lifetime within a company, so it is not surprising that the announcement of a group move will be an immense shock to the majority of employees. The Price Waterhouse/CBI Employee Relocation Council survey[1] however, found that some organizations reported that staff accepted the relocation easily as 'just another change' in a series of changes. The survey commented that: 'Where organizations have a culture where changes in structure, individual positions and locations are endemic then corporate relocation should be accepted more readily. Typically these organizations will have high numbers of staff who move location as part of career progression.'

However, although management staff and high fliers may expect a relocation at some point in their careers, especially if the company they work for has a number of branches and there is a history of moving managerial staff, the prospect of a company relocation presents a different picture, without individual promotions to soften the blow.

A mobility culture that encourages individuals to change job and relocate is little help when it comes to a group move. It is also extremely difficult for a company to promote the idea of moving before the decision has been taken without raising suspicions and rumour and thus jeopardizing the move's chances of success.

However, once the announcement concerning relocation has been made, the company needs to promote the concept of mobility. This applies equally in cases where companies announce the decision to relocate before determining the new location and when organizations make their location decision before the announcement is made to employees. The promotion of a mobility culture depends on the communication of the relocation exercise. The better-informed employees are, the more likely they are to understand and accept the need for change and the greater their willingness to relocate.

As explained in Chapter 1, employees' willingness to move depends on a trade off between internal company factors and external environment, home life and social factors. If the employee's prospects within the company together with the external considerations outweigh the advantages of staying behind, finding another job and maintaining current lifestyle, then reloca- tion may appear attractive. However, employers need to be aware that a group move often presents more of a threat to employees (job or no job) than the opportunity offered by an individual transfer (promotion or no promotion).

Employees are always sensitive to change and are likely to be more so when relocation is taking place. Involving employees in the process of change and encouraging the interchange of information helps to develop a mobility culture. The encourage- ment of a team spirit among employees ('we're all in it together') helps to foster cooperation and a positive attitude towards moving.

Managing change
An organization's culture is influenced by a number of variables. These include not only the characteristics of the location itself but also organization structure and job design, systems, processes, management style, people and specific groups and history.

The relocation of an organization provides an opportunity to change these but to do so, employers must manage the change in culture. Objectives must be set and an integrated plan determined. Through this the core relocation message can be promoted and other worthwhile objectives met as well, for instance the intro- duction of technology, integration of linked functions and improved communications.

The key to managing a change in culture lies in communication with employees and in employee involvement. Where possible groups of employees should be involved in the aspects of the plan which directly affect them. Also it is crucial that a clear overall picture of what is to be achieved is determined. With this in mind, employees can see and understand the context in which changes are made.

Managing change at Shell Chemicals
In September 1986, Shell Chemicals UK announced the move of its head office from London to Chester and by December 1987 the move was complete. The management of the relocation of the head office was considered by the company as being synonymous with the management of change. The success of the move was related to the company's strong vision of its future – what it was doing and why. Shell Chemicals' vision was concerned with its

business strategy, namely to be located nearer to the company's manufacturing sites and customers.

The company developed its mobility culture through a number of positive actions. First, management received a clear mandate from those in authority to enable them to act decisively. A core team of five people committed to the change were responsible for ensuring that the physical aspects of the move took place (that the new building was built, that the staff moved home and that the office services were in place on the due date). Line managers committed to the move played a crucial role in developing the mobility culture. To begin with, reaction to the move was negative (as would be expected) but a consistent and unified management message that there was no alternative to relocation caused employees to change their views, to stop questioning why the move was necessary, and to think instead of how it could be done. Low morale was turned around and enthusiasm and team spirit resulted. There was considerable staff involvement in the design and layout of the new office and the furniture, fittings and office service arrangements. The short timetable for the move (about 15 months) gave staff less time to question the principles behind it or how it could be carried out in a different way. The relocation also prompted the introduction of new technology and improvement to working arrangements.

Enthusiasm for relocation and the excitement of the change dies away after the move is complete. Shell Chemicals' management was prepared for this and implemented a programme of activities, including customer visits to the new office, which demonstrated the benefits of the move. As part of the official opening, a video was produced to be shown to company visitors to explain the move and staff's reactions to it. This approach raised Shell Chemicals' profile in the media as well, it resulted in considerable coverage for both the company and the employees themselves, thus maintaining the excitement of the move and continued employee involvement. There was also a major 'Welcome to Chester' dinner dance for all staff and their partners to thank them for all their help and cooperation and give everyone a chance to let their hair down and celebrate the successful move.

Planning the move

Planning is crucial to the success of a relocation exercise and care must be taken to ensure that all details are covered. Relocation is a very emotive subject so management needs to have answers to employees' questions ready once the move is announced. It is also important at this stage to determine a timetable, to ensure an ordered sequence of events later on.

The timescale for a group move is usually between one and three years from planning to completion. For example, when Digital moved an operation from Reading to Fareham, the company planned the relocation exercise for one year and then allowed for a second period of one year for implementation.

When The Law Society decentralized part of its functions from London to Redditch, the project took a year to complete. The sequence of events was as follows:

- in June 1987 staff consultations began
- in September 1987 the search began
- in December 1987 the decision to decentralize was taken
- in January 1988 the premises were acquired
- in April 1988 the first staff moved in
- by July 1988 the move was completed.

When Shell Chemicals UK relocated its head office from London to Chester, the relocation process took 15 months from the decision to relocate to full occupation of the new premises. And when NEC Electronics (UK) moved its administration headquarters from Motherwell to Milton Keynes in 1986, the relocation process was scheduled to take 18 months to organize and execute; it actually took 15 months in total.

Some companies allow longer timescales: Reader's Digest, for example, is allowing three years for its project to move a division of around 200 people from London to Swindon.

One of the main problems which companies face is that of delays to their planned schedule. Firms usually plan to carry out the physical move during quiet times in their business cycles. Delays can mean that staff have to move during the busiest part of the year and can also result in unforseen costs.

In the Price Waterhouse/CBI Employee Relocation Council survey[1] of company moves 'the most frequently encountered problem was delays, mostly associated with the provision of new accommodation, caused by unforseen conditions, difficulties with building contractors and in the supply of specialist plant and equipment'. Other reasons for the delays experienced by companies included the supply and installation of new telecommunications facilities, delays in obtaining grants and financial incentives and in gaining planning permission. The delivery and installation of new technology also resulted in delays.

Employee profiles
An important part of the relocation planning stage is to gather information on the current workforce and to determine labour needs in the new location. Personnel records may prove to be of limited use in attempting to understand employee's personal circumstances and gauge whether they are likely to move, as they are often out of date. Often companies collect data on marital status and children only when the employee is recruited, although some do update records annually as part of the appraisal process. However, it is unlikely that personnel records will show whether the employee's spouse works, let alone give details on the spouse's career. Personnel records should show where employees live and from this employers may be able to gain some idea as to how many staff will agree to relocate or if any could commute to the new location. For example, when Rank Xerox moved its headquarters out of central London, Marlow was chosen out of around 100 sites which were under consideration. Around 60 per cent of the staff already lived within a 30 mile radius of the new location.

By using information on areas in which employees live, employers can establish their likely house prices and these can be compared with prices in the new area. Schools and sporting facilities could also be studied and old compared with new. At this stage in the planning process, companies should decide who is to be offered relocation assistance and on what terms and who is to be offered redundancy. The relocation/redundancy packages may be structured to provide generous relocation provisions to employees whom the company wishes to relocate and perhaps a better redundancy package to those it does not want to move. A cost effective balance is required. Plans to provide cover to maintain operations up to and beyond the date of the move should also be made.

Predicting the number of employees who will move with any degree of accuracy is difficult. As a result, employers often have only a general idea of how many new staff they will require in the new location and of the skills required. However, some general assumptions can be made – lower graded employees are less likely to relocate and female clerical and secretarial staff are also unlikely to move, especially if they provide the lower second income to their household and if similar jobs are plentiful in their home areas.

Nevertheless, to plan for continuity of operations employers do need to judge fairly accurately the numbers who will agree to move. It is difficult to probe for information on employees' circumstances without creating rumours, especially if management has decided that confidentiality is to be maintained before the official relocation announcement.

If the planning stage is well advanced, even though the final location has not been decided, it may prove worthwhile to conduct an employee attitude survey to find out staffs' preferences. For example, when Phillips Petroleum decided to relocate from central London, it had eight potential sites under consideration including Croydon, Wembley, Hammersmith and Woking. Phillips analysed where employees lived and conducted a survey to see where they wanted to go.

However, if such a survey is carried out the results need to be followed up, otherwise staff may feel that their opinions are not valued by the company and this may undermine the whole exercise.

Location research

In the early planning stage the company should decide why the move is necessary, determine goals and draw up site selection criteria. A number of locations may emerge which satisfy these. It is then necessary to examine local characteristics of importance to the company – such as communications and skills availability – and to the employees – such as housing, schooling, transport and leisure facilities.

If a consultant has not already been employed to determine the relocation goals and site characteristics, this is the time when many companies do call on specialist outside help to research their chosen areas in depth. Consultants can provide profiles of housing types and costs, transport links to the new premises, schooling types and availability, leisure facilities, etc. Research into the labour market can provide valuable data to employers and research into the possibility of company expansion is also important. The choice of location can also present a particular image of the company to potential customers and employees which may be of importance to the employer.

Location research can be especially time consuming. Whoever conducts this research, whether it is a consultant or a member of staff, must be open-minded and be aware of the dangers of making subjective judgements.

Company objectives have to be met and the new location should meet the desired criteria. However, to encourage employees to relocate, the area must also meet their needs. In researching the characteristics of the new site, it is advisable to compare these with where employees currently live so that management will have answers prepared and facts ready when employees ask the inevitable questions about housing, cost of living, schools and so on.

This research stage of the planning process is not, however, as straightforward as it sounds. Research into housing costs and availability, and the labour market will provide only a snapshot of the current state of the market. Over time these factors will change and the results may prove harmful to the relocation's chances of success. For example, house prices may rise and, once the announcement of a large company move is public knowledge, house prices in the new area are bound to increase. The labour market may change, especially if other companies are moving into the area and want to employ local people.

For example, when Reader's Digest relocated part of its mailing · services department from London to Swindon in 1980, labour in the area was relatively plentiful. Although in 1989, its current relocation operation of the remainder of the department makes sound economic sense in terms of reducing office rents, the labour market in Swindon is now very tight and the company anticipates recruitment difficulties, as many companies in the area have unfilled vacancies. Also, over the three year timescale of the move, house prices have risen to the extent that for some staff, house purchase will be impossible and council housing will be the only option.

Changes in the local employment market proved to be a problem for many of the companies interviewed in the Price Waterhouse/CBI Employee Relocation Council survey.[1] Salary differentials between the old and new locations closed and the recruitment of good, loyal staff was considered difficult. The survey found these problems to be particularly apparent in Peterborough and Milton Keynes.

Confidentiality
During the planning process, the majority of companies believe that confidentiality is the best policy. If there are rumours of a potential move, staff are likely to be anxious about their futures, worried about losing their jobs and the effects of moving on their families. Rumours spread fast and result in discontent. Some staff may even seek other jobs merely as a result of believing unconfirmed, possibly false, information. As a result it is common practice for only a small team to be involved in the planning process and for secrecy to be maintained either until the final location is known or until a short-list of locations has been determined. At NEC Electronics UK, for example, the decision making for the move was carried out by a small, select team of three managers working with external consultants. All the details of the move were kept confidential until the announcement took place, after which the relocation exercise took six months to implement.

Maintaining confidentiality is, without doubt, a major problem in planning a relocation. Companies may benefit from involving managers and others within the organization by using their knowledge and experience, but the greater the number of people in the project team, the more likely the chance of leaked information. The need to keep plans secret also puts pressure on those involved in the relocation planning stage, as they need to balance their own concerns about the relocation and the impact on their families with the demands of the company.

Employment law

When planning a company move, the employment law implications need to be considered. First, the employees' contracts of employment must be examined. How the contract of employment defines place of work determines whether employees are entitled to redundancy payments and may play a part in determining fair or unfair dismissal.

If the contract of employment states that the place of work is at a particular premises then, generally speaking, any relocation to another site without the employee's consent will result in a breach of contract.

Some contracts of employment, however, do not specifically state a place of work but instead contain a mobility clause. This gives the employer the right to transfer employees to another site without breaching employees' contracts. Widely drawn mobility clauses enable employers to require employees to relocate without risking constructive dismissal. However, they may be interpreted as being indirectly discriminatory if one sex is put at a disadvantage disproportionately as a result of the mobility clause.

The contract of employment cannot be 'silent on the place of work'. If there is no express term in the contract referring to place of work, such a term is implied. The degree of mobility that may be implied often depends on the circumstances of the case. However, it is common for the courts to imply a term in employees' contracts that they be prepared to work in other locations, particularly if they are employed in a 'mobile' industry group (for instance construction) or if the relocation is to a site within reasonable daily commuting distance.

If an employee refuses to relocate, this may be considered to be a fair reason for dismissal (subject to the general requirement of reasonableness). The grounds for dismissal may be redundancy (if the employer's proposed move results in a variation of the place of work as defined in the employee's contract of employment) or misconduct (if the contract contains a mobility clause which gives the employer the right to transfer the individual).

Employers are considered to have good business reasons for relocating (they would not consider doing so if it was not thought to be in their best interest) and hence tribunals would not normally question why a company moves or the commercial reasons behind the relocation. However, they do question the fairness of the dismissal and the procedures followed by employers in carrying it out.

In cases of redundancy, employers must follow redundancy procedures by giving advance warning and consulting before any decision to dismiss employees is taken. The same principles apply when the dismissal is a result of misconduct, although a refusal to move may be treated as a disciplinary matter.

Consultation is considered necessary so that employers and employees have the opportunity to find a mutually acceptable solution which meets the needs of both of them. By establishing the employee's objections to the move, it may be possible for them to be resolved, thus eliminating the need for dismissal. If the differences cannot be solved, the employee is entitled to redundancy pay and the employer must consult with any recognized trade unions on the redundancies. Although employees are *prima facie* entitled to redundancy pay, they may lose this right if they unreasonably refuse an offer of suitable alternative employment.

The suitability of the alternative employment is judged from the employer's side; the reasonableness of the refusal from the employee's side. So, for instance, if suitable alternative employment is offered in the new location but acceptance of the job is dependent on the employee moving home, refusal to accept is unlikely to be considered unreasonable. But if it is possible to commute to the new location, then turning down the job may be considered unreasonable. However, the employee's personal circumstances may be important here. If the new location is within reasonable commuting distance but the employee cannot combine travel requirements with, for instance, the care of dependent relatives, refusal to accept the offer of suitable alternative employment may be considered reasonable. The level of financial/practical help offered by the employer is also taken into account by tribunals in reaching their decision. Employees have the right to try out the new job for a four week trial period before reaching a final decision.

Allowances

Relocation allowances packages offered to employees involved in a group move are generally similar to those offered in cases of individual transfers. However, promotional increases in pay are not generally included in the package and so companies may pay higher disturbance allowances for a group move than for individual transfers to help compensate. Indeed, employees may find their salaries reduced on relocation, for instance, if they lose area allowances as a result of the move. It is usual, therefore, for area weighting payments to be phased out gradually over up to a four year period (maximum).

For those commuting to the new location, commuting allowances are generally paid to help offset increased travel costs. Again, these tend to reduce over time and are usually paid for up to a maximum of four years. Commuting allowances are taxable but a few companies gross them up for tax. Car purchase loan schemes may be introduced into the allowances package to help those opting to commute.

The allowances package for a group move also usually contains some form of bonus payment for staff who are to be made redundant to encourage them to stay with the company up to the date of the move. This normally amounts to between 10 per cent and 15 per cent of salary but may be as much as 25 per cent of salary.

Implementing the move

Once the planning stage of the move is completed, the second major phase is to implement the plan. The first step is to make the announcement to staff.

Announcing the relocation

The announcement of a relocation exercise will have a dramatic effect on staff. It will be a major emotional shock so it is crucial to plan it properly: first impressions count.

The form of the announcement may be as a management presentation and/or via written material, audio/visual material. The method and timing will affect staff reactions, so, as far as possible, groups of staff should receive the announcement at the same time and the message should be consistent for each group.

If a presentation is to be given, venues need to be organized. The speaker should appear confident and decisive, be able to handle questions and provide a clear message. The announcement must cover which staff are affected, where staff are to move and when, the reasons behind the relocation and the help which will be given to those who are moving and those who are not.

The shock of the announcement may be so great that staff do not remember any detailed points clearly, so written information should be provided to staff at the time that the announcement is made. Staff will need to supply information to their families and so will require information in a form that they can take home. Documentation must be worded carefully and legal issues considered before publication.

To assist in the presentation of information, video or slide shows may be used. This method of communciation is particularly useful if the announcement is to be made at different company locations at the same time, because it ensures a consistent message to staff.

The content of the announcement depends on who is being asked to move and who is being made redundant. If everyone is to be offered relocation, detailed information can be given on the relocation package. If some staff are to be made redundant, only a summary of redundancy/relocation benefits can be given at this stage. Follow-up meetings with individuals and/or groups are necessary.

The timing of the announcement is important. Presentations should be made early in the morning to ensure enough time during the day for any necessary follow-up meetings and for employees to have time to ask questions. During the day employees must gain a full understanding of what the relocation means to them. Information must be given on the new location, on the relocation allowances package and on the redundancy provisions. Each employee should be given an information pack, perhaps even a copy of the video on the new area to take home.

Period before the move
It helps if, during the period before the move, communications are good between staff and management. Periods of indecision and little or no communication invariably reduce morale, so management must be attentive to the needs of two groups of employees – the movers and the stayers – and to provide assistance and advice on a wide range of issues. Both financial and practical help is needed. However, employee involvement and communication provide the key to success.

Communication techniques checklist

The following list of communication techniques can be used for those staff who are relocating with the company:

- An information room inside the company with displays of maps and up-to-date housing information. Estate agents could be invited to make presentations on housing in the new area.
- An information kit or pack for employees to take home with user-friendly local information and allowance details.
- The use of videos or film shows to portray the new area, schools, housing, etc. Videos may also be made to explain the allowances policy. Videos could be made available for employees to take home.
- Slide shows could be used to present a visual impression of the new area – less expensive to produce than videos.
- Informal evenings or lunches could be arranged with families

invited into the company to listen to presentations and ask questions.

● A company newspaper or newsletter could be published to report on the relocation and current developments.

● Coach trips could be organized to take employees and their spouses, possibly whole families, to visit the new area to see the new work location, local amenities, housing, etc. Free time should be provided for exploring the area.

● If possible, employers should make use of employees who already live or work at the new location. Arrange for them to meet groups of prospective transferees to answer questions.

● One person in the company needs to be responsible for co-ordinating the information campaign. Lines of communication must be clear: in this way, when employees have questions, they can be sure whom to ask to get answers.

● Regular briefing meetings should be run so employees are kept up-to-date with progress. Line managers may be used effectively in this way.

● Personal counselling can be provided to assist employees on a one-to-one basis with their individual relocation concerns.

Non-movers

The staff who decide not to relocate must not be forgotten. They must understand clearly the terms offered to them (redundancy, retention bonuses payable if they agree to work for certain periods to maintain continuity of operations, etc). Consultation with unions may be necessary and to some extent this may determine the approach taken by the company. If alternative employment is offered, the correct legal procedure must be followed.

Those leaving the company need not feel neglected. Their dissatisfaction may reduce employee morale and productivity: the staff will be concerned about their future. The use of experienced counsellors may help them determine their career priorities and find placements elsewhere.

Follow-up

Employers need to follow up on employees' concerns right through to the date of the move and beyond. On the day of the move, a small gesture from the company can go a long way towards improving morale – a small gift delivered to the employee's new home or awaiting them on their desk at work provides a personal touch which shows that the company cares. Once the move has taken place, the employees' excitement and enthusiasm may die away. Management should try to maintain this enthusiasm, to keep morale – and productivity – high once the new building is occupied.

Case studies

The following brief case studies of company moves illustrate the points made in this chapter. The selection indicates the approaches used by companies in various situations: moves from north to south and vice versa as well as long distance and short distance moves. Further information on many of these case studies may be obtained through references given in the bibliography.

Timeplex Ltd – relocation from Leeds and Brentford to Langley
Timeplex Ltd was launched in the UK in 1980. The company is a wholly-owned UK subsidiary of Timeplex Incorporated which is based in New Jersey in the USA, specializing in data communications. Leeds was chosen as the head office location because of its good motorway, rail and air links as well as its proximity to Leeds University – a good source of science and technology graduates. The company's second office was located in Brentford, West London. Its function was to penetrate southern business activity.

By 1985, the company's order book had swelled and a third office was opened in Livingstone to develop business in Scotland. By 1986, turnover had grown to £15 million and the number of staff employed had risen from six to around 140. Shortage of space was proving to be a major problem at the Brentford office and the Leeds office was also becoming cramped. In addition to this, about 70 per cent of the company's customers were based in the south of England. The company decided that new premises were needed in addition to the Scottish and Leeds facilities, in place of the Brentford location. The new office had to be southern based and the Leeds head office function was to be moved to this new site to serve the customer base.

Timeplex also decided that the new premises had to be housed in a new, prestigious building which would project the right company image. It had to be based in a good location, too, close to London (but without commuting problems), have good communications links with the north of Britain as well as beyond the UK, and it had to be located in an area with a good quality of life. Langley, near Slough, was chosen, as it met these requirements.

The initial planning stage was carried out in total secrecy, with only senior management involved. The company did not want rumour and unrest to be created when no final decision had been made.

The company did not have a personnel department at this stage and so the relocation of personnel was handled by senior management. In planning the process, the principles involved in moving people who worked in the affected departments were addressed at the beginning. Guidelines were established early on which could be used for the relocation of personnel. The company believed that the staff working in Brentford would welcome the news, as they could escape from the misery of commuting. Most of them already lived to the west of London and Langley is a mile from the M4 and the M25; the M3 and M40 are close by and so no travel problems for this group were envisaged. However, the company realized that relocating staff from Leeds might cause difficulties. Staff would have to leave their native areas, their families and friends and move 200 miles south to an unknown area with high house prices.

Timeplex's philosophy is that its greatest asset is its people. The company wanted its staff to share in its success and to retain their skills, abilities and talents. Having decided that it wanted to take all staff in affected departments to the new location, the next stage in the planning process was to determine the effects on staff and how the move should be presented and announced. Management meetings were held to discuss how to alleviate staffs' concerns, where people could live, what house prices were, how quality of life could be maintained, the items which should be included in the relocation allowances package, comparable salaries in the new location and available outside third party assistance.

Timeplex's management also tried to analyse the personal circumstances of each employee affected – for example whether they had a working spouse and whether they had dependent relatives. From this information, attempts were made to project how many people would move. During this analysis, outside professional help was brought in to assist in the preparation of the announcement to staff. Black Horse Relocation was engaged to provide a guaranteed home sale scheme to help homeowners to move quickly and easily. National Startpoint produced information guides on the Langley area and nearby locations to assist staff in choosing an area to live.

A placement agency was also hired to help find employment for spouses and/or relatives of employees moving to Langley and to find employment in Leeds for Timeplex staff not moving south. The placement agency was briefed to provide assistance to non-movers with advice on marketing themselves for jobs, including preparation of a CV, writing letters, telephone techniques and personal presentation.

Timplex management worked with Black Horse Relocation to determine a relocation allowances package and to present it as a printed guide. The package covered househunting expenses for three trips for the employee and family, estate agents' fees, legal costs, removal costs, temporary accommodation or temporary commuting costs, a 10 per cent of salary payment as a disturbance allowance, plus bridging loan interest. An excess housing cost allowance scheme was also included in the package. Under this, the company paid the mortgage interest differential on a house for three years where evaluations increased by up to 100 per cent between the old and the new property values. Reimbursement of loss on sale was also included in the package, if enforced quick sales were necessary for employees to move quickly.

Staff affected by the move were the southern sales and field service from Brentford, and product engineering, technical assistance centre and repair, marketing, finance and group services staff from Leeds. Those unaffected were the Scottish office staff and the Leeds-based northern sales, field service and operations personnel.

To make the announcement, management decided to use a company presentation rather than departmental briefings. Hotels were booked in the north and the south, and staff were invited to attend. (Company presentations were frequently held in hotels so this did not raise suspicion beforehand.) The first announcement was made to all the Leeds based staff in early April 1986. The managing director began the presentation by explaining the reasons for the move, the role of the employees within the company and why the company wanted all employees in affected departments to relocate. Understanding of why employees might not want to move for personal reasons was also demonstrated. Established company principles were re-stated – namely that Timeplex is a full employment company and that it intended to maintain employees' quality of life.

The information packages covering financial implications, the new location, educational and recreation facilities were distributed.

Once the announcement had been given, employees were able to split up into departmental groups where department heads gave slide presentations providing more detail. In this informal atmosphere, employees could ask questions. Follow-up meetings were then announced for the following week, when employees' families could attend.

The announcement meetings were held early on a Friday afternoon, leaving ample time for questions. Employees could go home afterwards to give the general information to their families. Each employee was given a list of all the management's home addresses and telephone numbers and every manager was available to answer questions or have private discussions. The same presentation was given to the southern-based staff on the following Monday at a southern hotel.

At the Leeds follow-up meetings, consultants from Black Horse Relocation and National Startpoint, along with Timeplex management, presented detailed information to families and answered questions.

The move to the new location was phased with the Brentford staff and some of the Leeds-based departments moving between May and July 1986. The second phase took place between May and August 1987 and involved the group services and financial departments from Leeds.

Timeplex considers the relocation exercise to have been very successful. No staff were made redundant and no staff underwent even a short period of unemployment. Everyone either moved south, were re-deployed in the Leeds office or found employment with other companies in the area. A measure of the company's success was that two married women working for the company persuaded their husbands (who were the main wage earners) to move south. Since moving south, the company's order book has more than doubled.

Digital – relocation from Reading to Fareham
In July 1988 Digital moved a £60 million business unit from Reading to Fareham. The company decided to move because a south coast location complemented its regional structure. The move involved over 200 employees and their families. All staff from secretaries to senior managers were offered full relocation provisions, including a guaranteed home sale scheme from the relocation management company PHH Homequity.

In preparing for the relocation exercise, the company identified four major action areas: planning; involvement; communication; and ownership. The planning cycle took 24 months from initiation to implementation – 12 months before the move and an implementation stage for 12 months after the move. A member of the management team was appointed as a full-time relocation manager for the project. The company has a participative style of management and so involvement was key to the project.

The announcement was made at an introductory presentation, followed by group seminars covering finance and home sale. Each employee saw a video about the move and received a detailed information pack to take home. The company also set up a property corner and a home sale hotline. Trips were arranged to visit the new site with a surprise helicopter trip over the new location. Employees and their partners could share their concerns and ask questions. Counselling sessions were held, along with a series of coffee evenings to help provide information to employees and their spouses.

The relocation allowances package applying to moves within the company (Digital relocates some 140 existing employees a year) was amended to increase the miscellaneous allowance. Digital also took steps to assist employees obtain jobs for spouses in the new location.

The company wanted to ensure that all the processes and procedures adopted involved equal 'ownership' by employees and managers, so all policies were interactive. The success of the relocation has been measured by a 30 per cent growth in business after the relocation took place.

STC Telecommunications – relocation from North London to Harlow
STC Telecommunications is part of the STC Group of companies. It is a leading international telecommunications company. During 1986, the company determined that, if it was to exploit its technological lead in multiplexing systems and intelligent network management, it would need to achieve about a 50 per cent growth in the engineering resource by the end of 1986. However, the company was having difficulty in recruiting professional systems designers, software and electronic engineers to work in the New Southgate headquarters location. Applicants attended interviews and seemed keen to work for STC but, despite competitive relocation, salary and benefit packages, many were rejecting job offers.

The company concluded that these people could not afford to

live in the suburbs of North London or in South Hertfordshire. So it decided to set up a satellite engineering operation in a lower cost housing area, to move key staff to this site and then put the growth of the satellite plant into operation, while continuing to recruit at New Southgate. Locations considered for the satellite site were Stevenage (where the group already had an established operation), Hemel Hempstead, Luton, Milton Keynes and Harlow.

With the opening of the M25, Harlow became the company's first choice. STC already had its components, optic fibre and research operations established there and so the company found space in the same area for its new technical centre.

Some 50 key staff involved in the relocation were given counselling sessions on the move and a recruitment campaign began in Harlow and in New Southgate, with the intention of recruiting a further 70 people to work at the new site. Senior technical staff were offered the opportunity of home relocation; junior and support staff were offered travel assistance.

To qualify for a relocation of their homes, the company's policy was that the single journey from the current home to Harlow had to be either 15 miles more than to New Southgate, or the single journey be at least 10 miles more with the total daily travel exceeding 25 miles. All mileages were measured by the shortest practicable route. The location of the new house also had materially to reduce home-to-work journey time.

The relocation allowances package included: the costs of estate agents' and legal fees to a maximum of £2,500; removal costs; survey fees up to £300; mortgage guarantee premium and mortgage redemption charge; bridging loan interest for 13 weeks and a disturbance allowance depending on circumstances to a maximum of £3,500. Temporary commuting costs for up to 26 weeks of 23p per mile were also paid (taxable). The relocation package was paid in the form of an interest-free loan, to be cancelled after two years if the employee remained with the company. Leavers had to repay their loan on a pro-rata basis. (The loan was reduced by one twenty-fourth for each month of service after the date the loan was granted.)

Staff not relocating received reimbursement of additional commuting costs incurred, paid in full in the first year, reducing by 25 per cent per annum and ceasing on the fourth anniversary of the job transfer.

The company also introduced a car loan scheme to help staff requiring new vehicles to drive to work. The company made loans available of up to £2,000. Loans did not exceed 60 per cent of the purchase price of the vehicle. If the employee stayed with the company for at least two years from the start of the loan, it was written off with no payment required. Those employees leaving within two years were required to repay the loan on a pro-rata basis. Of the 46 staff who transferred their base location to Harlow, four moved home and 42 opted to commute. Twenty of these took the option of the car loan.

The timetable for product development is on schedule and recruitment has become easier. The company believes that the relocation exercise was worthwhile.

Rank Xerox – relocation from London to Marlow
In 1984, Rank Xerox International Headquarters had a number of sites in the London area – Euston Road in London, Bushey, Aylesbury and Uxbridge. The company wanted to consolidate these and thus save travelling time between sites, rates and running costs. It also wanted to create a high quality working environment and to project a high quality image. It was too expensive to refurbish the Euston Road headquarters and to introduce new technology into it. Rates on the Euston Road building were also considered to be very expensive and were rising. So management decided to find a site outside London with good transport links.

Out of 100 sites considered, Marlow was eventually chosen. The location enables Rank Xerox to reduce its costs by around 50 per cent and more than double available space. In addition, 60 per cent of the company's staff already lived within a 30 mile radius of the site.

In January 1984, the company issued a booklet which outlined the proposed move, who was eligible for relocation plus information on Marlow. This was updated in 1986. Feature articles were published in the company's magazine and eight special supplements were brought out to cover the stages of the construction of the new building. Roadshows began, with personnel staff visiting company locations to present information on relocation allowances and the Marlow area generally. Personnel managers were available to answer questions from staff and discuss individual cases.

Rank Xerox developed a new relocation policy for the Marlow move. This included reasonable legal costs (0.5 per cent of sale and purchase costs), reasonable estate agents' fees, two building society survey fees and removal costs. Temporary accommodation was allowed for up to 13 weeks and a disturbance allowance was paid of 12.5 per cent of salary to homeowners; 10 per cent for first time buyers; and 7.5 per cent for those moving to and from rented property. Alternatively, employees could take a £2,000 lump sum.

For those choosing not to relocate, incremental travel costs were paid. This amounted to the difference between current costs and the projected cost of travel to Marlow. Employees could either receive this as an up-front lump sum for car purchase or have it in two equal instalments, a year apart. The company also decided to run a bus service to the Marlow site.

A guaranteed home sale scheme was available through two relocation companies: employees could choose which to use. Bridging loans were available interest-free to those using a relocation company, and interest-free for six months only to others. An additional housing cost allowance scheme was also given. Employees leaving within 12 months of the relocation of the company were asked to repay their relocation expenses on a pro-rata basis.

Rank Xerox's move was staggered. The move began in January 1987 and ended in April. Because of this, staff who moved later were not affected by the full impact of the clawback provisions when they left the company, as the pro-rata repayment referred to the date of the company move rather than the employee's personal move.

On arrival at the new building, staff received a letter of welcome and an invitation to a cocktail party in the staff restaurant that day.

The company's move was not without its problems. Despite mobility clauses in their contracts of employment, a few staff claimed redundancy, took their cases to tribunal and won. However, the company lodged an appeal at the Employment Appeals Tribunal (EAT) and the tribunal decision was overturned.

The Marlow site is some distance from shops and local transport is poor. As a result the company runs a bus service into Marlow town at considerable cost.

However, the move has been regarded as successful. Only 18 people out of a total workforce of 800 declined to work in the new location. The company's objectives have been met – staff are working in an advanced environment and the consolidation of activities has been achieved. The rate of growth is such that the company is currently looking for an additional site.

NEC Electronics (UK) Ltd – relocation from Motherwell to Milton Keynes

NEC is an international company with four main divisions – communications, computers, home electronics and electron devices. NEC Electronics (UK) Ltd is responsible for sales, marketing and distribution of the electron device group; semiconductor sales account for about 70 per cent of NEC Electronics' sales revenue. Products in the industry are becoming more complex and the market for them, more competitive.

In 1985, NEC Electronics (UK) Ltd had its administration headquarters, warehouse and Scottish sales office in Motherwell, with regional sales offices in Dublin, Reading and Birmingham. The headquarters was considered to be too remote from its customers and the company decided that it needed its sales teams closer to its customers. It decided to relocate the Motherwell head office function and the Birmingham and Reading organizations into one consolidated site at Milton Keynes. The Motherwell site would remain as a warehouse and distribution centre and the Dublin office would be unaffected by the move.

In determining the new location, the company wanted to be centrally based, a maximum of one and a half to two hours drive from customers and with Heathrow in easy reach. Because the company wanted a speedy relocation process (any longer than six months from the date of announcement was considered difficult to manage), a building had to be readily available.

The decision-making for the move was carried out by a small, select group of three managers who decided to use external consultants to help with the relocation. Details of the proposed move were kept secret until the announcement as it was felt that uncertainty would result in rumour and discontent. The company recognized that key members of staff would not be prepared to relocate if their families were anxious and worried. The company, therefore, placed considerable emphasis on domestic concerns and took great care to balance company requirements against the needs of employees.

When the time came to announce the relocation to staff (less than one year after the decision to move was taken), the company had determined exactly where the new location would be, who was affected by the move and when it would take place. Reasons for moving were prepared to give a full and frank explanation to staff. After the announcement an open evening was held, during which staff from the Milton Keynes Development Corporation advised on housing and schooling in the area. Employment counselling was made available to spouses and older children leaving school. A relocation package was offered with redundancy available as an option. Two weekend visits were arranged and, after the second visit to Milton Keynes, staff were asked to decide whether they would relocate.

Over 80 per cent of the employees affected agreed to move to Milton Keynes. The move was phased with the Motherwell headquarters staff moving first, followed by the Reading staff and lastly those from Birmingham. From the date of the public announcement the relocation was accomplished in under six months, with the planning and implementation stages together taking a total of 15 months.

The company is pleased with the success of the relocation exercise. Since the move, staff turnover has been low, with only one person leaving to go back to Scotland. Feedback from staff has been good and the company finds it easier to recruit young graduates and other professional staff.

However, the loyalty of new recruits is not as high as before and turnover amongst these people is greater than the company experienced in Scotland. Nevertheless, business has grown from £35 million after two and a half years in Milton Keynes and investment has continued in Motherwell to increase the capacity of the Scottish warehouse facility.

Shell Chemicals UK – relocation from London to Chester
Shell Chemicals' decision to relocate from central London to Chester was the result of numerous factors. The Northumberland Avenue site was cramped and unsuitable for the introduction of new technology. It also did not present a suitable image. Rather than move to Shell-Mex House in London, the company wanted to emphasize its own corporate identity. It also wanted to be nearer to its manufacturing bases in Cheshire and closer to its customers. The company's finance department was already at Wilmslow, so Chester was chosen as an area where the company could have a purpose built office on a greenfield site.

Staff were sent a circular in July 1986 telling them that the company had begun to search for a new head office site. This was followed up by articles in the company magazine and regular progess reports.

Head office employees, managerial and technical staff would be required to move to Chester. Shell Chemicals gave general managers the job of determining the staffing profiles of their new departments in Chester and drawing up career paths for these staff. Between 80 and 90 per cent of these staff were offered employment in and relocation to Chester.

The move was announced officially in September 1986 with group briefings and a video produced for staff to take home. In November, job offers were made to those moving to Chester and the company set up a project team of five managers who had the responsibility of ensuring that the building was built, that the office services were installed and to handle the staff relocation. The company expected staff to be mobile and voluntary severance was not offered as an alternative to relocation. However, the company did make every effort to re-deploy non-movers in the Shell Group's London locations, and in the event succeeded in finding alternative jobs for all those who wanted them.

In January 1987 an information guide was produced and in February a series of presentations were made to staff by local representatives and specialists on housing, education and amenities in the Chester area. Videos on housing and education were available for employees to take home. These contained interviews with estate agents and Shell employees already living in the Chester area.

An information room was also established in Northumberland Avenue. This contained estate agents' details and other information on the new area. Visits were arranged for employees and their families to see the Chester area for one or two days. A fact-file of local information was given to each member of staff. Open evenings were run in London and employees were able to have appointments with relocation counsellors to discuss their concerns and the benefits available to them under the relocation package. Estate agents and local education authority officers were available to answer questions.

The househunting process began in April 1987 and by September the new building was ready. By this time 70 per cent of the staff who were going to relocate had found the accommodation that they wanted. By the middle of December 1987, everyone had begun work in the new location.

The relocation allowances package was generous and provided a variety of assistance. Staff whose jobs were to remain in Chester for at least 18 months were offered the options of sale and purchase, second property purchase or to retain their existing property in the south and rent an additional property.

For staff choosing the sale and purchase option, the following allowances were given:

- legal fees
- estate agents' fees
- stamp duty
- land registry charges
- structural survey and related fees
- bridging loan interest
- temporary accommodation for the family for 13 weeks plus associated costs
- rates, insurance, utility standing charges on vacated but unsold property plus gardening costs
- removal, travel and overnight hotel costs
- furnishings allowance as a percentage of basic salary
- loss on sale under guaranteed price scheme
- a taxable settling-in allowance
- school uniform costs plus losses on school fees
- visits home if old property unsold
- mortgage assistance payable over eight years.

Mortgage assistance was given to the value of either the guaranteed sale price or the actual sale price, whichever was the greater, plus the grade maximum of the relevant grade. Interest was paid on the difference in mortgage costs, reducing over eight years.

Employees opting for a second property purchase received: legal fees and stamp duty (based on the value of the guaranteed price); one structural survey and one mortgage valuation; temporary accommodation for the family for 13 weeks plus associated costs; removal and travel costs plus overnight accommodation. A furnishings allowance, settling-in allowance, school uniform fees and mortgage assistance were also available. The mortgage assistance was related to the salary-linked value minus the value of the current property.

Staff choosing to retain their existing home and rent another one received: legal and agents' fees; removal and travel costs and overnight hotel costs; temporary accommodation for the family for four weeks plus associated costs; furnishings allowance, settling-in allowance and school uniform/fees as above; rental assistance based on total cost, reducing over eight years but, if property was let, assistance was reduced.

Employees who were likely to spend less than 18 months in the new location and, more usually, those likely to be there for less than six months were offered relocation on a 'grass widow/er basis'. The assistance given amounted to: temporary accommodation for the employee for four weeks plus associated costs; settling-in allowance; continuation of a reduced London allowance; rental assistance over eight years as above; annual allowance towards other living costs; first class rail fares home at weekend plus meals in transit.

Employees living in rented accommodation received similar assistance to those employees choosing to retain their existing property and rent an additional home, although the rental assistance given amounted to the difference between the old and the new rental costs, reducing over eight years.

Shell Chemicals UK's move was completed in 15 months. Over 80 per cent of the staff offered relocation assistance moved with the company. After the exercise had been completed, a post-move follow-up video was made to record staffs' reactions to the move. The video is shown to many interested visitors to the new head office.

Reader's Digest – relocation from London to Swindon
Reader's Digest employs some 800 people in the UK. In 1980, the company moved its mailing services department (part of its fulfilment division) to Swindon. In 1988, the company announced a proposal to relocate the remainder of the fulfilment division, 200 people, to join the 200 employees already in Swindon. It planned to add a further 55,000 square feet of office accommodation to its existing department on its 11 acre site on the Blagrove Industrial Estate. The division consists of mailing services (200 people in Swindon) and the London-based computer services and systems development operation (50 people), the data centre (30 people) and customer services (120 people).

Reader's Digest took the decision to relocate for several reasons – the main one being the cost of office rent in central London (£48 per square foot in London compared with £8 per square foot in Swindon at 1988 prices). The annual savings were calculated at £2 million. The company decided to buy the Swindon site and, although this will increase the cost initially (£21 million will be spent on the land, the building and staff relocation), savings will be made in the medium-term. The company has calculated that there will be an adequate return on investment over 15 years.

The company believes that Swindon is ideally located for

distribution. The Blagrove Industrial Estate is close to the M4 and rail links to London are fast. There is also plenty of low cost space for access. When the firm relocated to Swindon in 1980, labour was plentiful and unemployment was high, as the British Rail engineering works had recently closed. However, by the time the second move was announced in January 1988, unemployment had fallen to 7 per cent. By mid-1989, the figure was only 4.7 per cent, so recruitment of staff is now likely to be more difficult.

The relocation project is planned to take three years. In July 1987 a relocation study was announced which was completed in December 1987. The move was announced in 1988 and staff were asked for their initial feelings about relocation and 38 per cent said that they were likely to move. Staff were given a year to reach a final decision. This would leave a further year for the company to recruit and train staff and for them to have 12 months in the job to become fully effective. Recruitment began in 1989 and may continue after the summer of 1990. The building work is being carried out during 1989 and the building should be fully equipped by May 1990. The company expects about 80 of its 200 staff to relocate and plans to recruit around 120 people in Swindon.

The information campaign to staff began with the announcement of the move. The fulfilment director invited all 200 staff to a lunchtime talk (four half hour sessions, each of 50 staff). The presentation explained the decision to move and the relocation offer. This announcement was followed with a two hour session which gave details on Swindon, the relocation package and the redundancy package. Information packs were distributed covering the details of the presentations. An exhibition was set up with information and displays on housing, education, arts and leisure. The exhibition was held in-company. Informal lunch and evening sessions were held while the exhibition was available so that staff could discuss their concerns. Tours were run to Swindon – 110 employees and 90 partners came on the coach day trip to Swindon. Every two months an information bulletin was published to report on the progress of the relocation.

Reader's Digest considered that listening to staff and involving them in the relocation was crucial to the success of the move. Line managers were appointed in a counselling role. Staff were involved in aspects of the move including plans for the new restaurant and sports and social club. Spouses were able to come to informal evening meetings. The 200 staff already in Swindon were also involved, as were the non-relocators. This enabled the company to understand staffs' concerns about the move. It emerged that partners' jobs were a worry for staff, although the high level of vacancies in Swindon did ease this problem. After the relocation was announced and as a result of the number of companies moving into the area, house prices rose by between 30 per cent and 40 per cent. This put house purchase beyond the reach of many first time buyers.

The company offered relocation assistance to all 200 employees, with generous redundancy payments as an alternative. The relocation package included:

- legal fees (solicitors' fees, stamp duty, etc)
- survey fees
- home sale assistance via a guaranteed home sale scheme
- home search assistance via Dow Sheppard Relocation
- house hunting visit costs
- removal costs
- a tax-free disturbance allowance to the maximum level allowed by the Inland Revenue plus a taxable percentage of salary
- any additional travel costs.

The move is still in progress. So far 31 employees have already moved or are in the process of doing so. The company believes that when the project is completed in 1990, its target will have been met.

Reference

1 PRICE WATERHOUSE *and* CBI EMPLOYEE RELOCATION COUNCIL. *Moving experiences*. London, Price Waterhouse and CBI Employee Relocation Council, 1989.

6

The European dimension

Although it is beyond the scope of this book to cover international relocation in detail, the impact of the Single European Market is likely to affect company approaches to both domestic and international relocation policies and practice. For this reason, this chapter – which draws on research (unpublished) carried out by the CBI Employee Relocation Council during the summer of 1989 – examines the impact of 1992 on relocation. The chapter reviews the practice of nine major organizations, diverse in their industry groups and products, their size and the origins of their parent companies. The organizations examined were:

Tioxide Group – a multi-national company with operations world-wide, although the largest sector of its business is in Europe. The company is the leading manufacturer of titanium pigments in Europe.

Digital Equipment Company – an American computer company operating world-wide.

Hogan Systems – an American company, specializing in computer software for the banking, insurance and finance sector.

BP – a major world-wide oil company.

Rhône-Poulenc Worldwide – a chemical company with pharmaceuticals as one of its specialities.

Willis Faber – a UK company with offices worldwide specializing in the international insurance and re-insurance broking market.

Reckitt & Colman – a UK-based organization which manufactures and markets branded consumer goods. Its main products are home and personal care items, pharmaceuticals, food, industrial pigments and artists' materials. The company has operations in every EEC country and in all continents.

Westland Helicopters – whose business is to research, develop and supply helicopters to the armed forces and overseas markets.

Grand Metropolitan – a UK company involved in the supply and distribution of food and drink as well as the restaurant and leisure business. With its recent takeover of Pillsbury, it now has a large US interest.

Responding to change

The majority of these organizations are instituting policies such as reorganization or rationalization; are opening new offices to gain a presence on the ground in Europe; or are actively involved in acquiring European companies as a direct response to the opportunities afforded by the Single European Market. Others are finding that the new business climate in Europe provides an ideal background in which to introduce and implement changes to established procedures.

For example, Reckitt & Colman is pursuing a programme of acquisitions and rationalization throughout Europe to explore the increased opportunities offered by the Single European Market. The plans involve the overall simplification and realignment of operations, concentrating on fewer activities to give a greater focus on core product lines. As part of these moves, the UK will manufacture some of the company's most successful European product lines, whilst others will be transferred from the UK to Reckitt & Colman sites around Europe.

Willis Faber specializes in the international insurance and re-insurance market. It already employs expatriate staff in three European locations. The company has recently acquired 20 per cent of a local direct broker in Belgium. This action is specifically geared to the approach of the Single European Market, with the aim of increasing the company's presence on the ground in Europe. It is considering plans to open an office in Brussels to which it will transfer a number of professionally qualified staff in order to coordinate plans for further expansion into Europe.

Rhône-Poulenc has production sites throughout Europe and 40 in France. The company finds that the Single European Market creates increased competition, especially from generic drug manu-facturers. As a result, the company is beginning a programme of acquisitions of small generic drug companies, both to reduce this competition and to respond to the market trend towards the use of generics.

Operating in a new climate

In contrast to these examples some organizations are not responding directly to the opportunities presented by 1992 but instead are indirectly taking advantage of the new business climate. At BP, for example, operations have traditionally been administered from the UK. In recent years, however, the company has set up two major centres within Europe to administer all European operations. A centre in Paris administers the Atlantic seaboard countries while a German centre administers other European, non-communist, BP operations. BP believes that there are many efficiencies to be gained through the creation of these supra-regional centres within Europe. For example, they assist in reducing duplication of activity. The approach of 1992 has not been the catalyst for this development although BP has found that the climate associated with 1992 has aided rationalization.

Effects on relocation

All this activity within Europe is likely to have a major effect on relocation policies and practice, recruitment and selection of expatriates and training of expatriate personnel. Already there is evidence of an increase in expatriation to Europe and a change in the mix of expatriate personnel. Currently, for example, Hogan Systems employs 10 expatriates in Europe. By 1992, the company envisages quadrupling this number.

BP employs 1,500 expatriates world-wide, of whom 1,200 are British. The company expects that this figure will change with fewer British expatriates (about 800 to 900) and more from other nationalities. Currently there are some 480 UK expatriates working in Europe and Scandinavia and the company expects that the overall number of people working in Europe will increase. There are also some 130 expatriates in Europe who work in a country outside their home base. BP expects that movement between European countries will increase and there will also be increased movement out of Europe to other locations in the world.

Reasons for expatriation

There are four main reasons for expatriation:

- to develop 'high fliers' for the top
- to fill skills gaps
- to transfer expertise and provide different experiences for senior and/or middle managers
- to develop new teams.

Developing people for the top

At Reckitt & Colman, for example, expatriation is an integral part of the career development process for those employees being groomed for higher management. When vacancies arise at senior level, the company looks world-wide for individuals with the necessary skills. Expatriation is also used to transfer expertise and to cross-fertilise product knowledge and ideas. At Rhône-Poulenc, British employees are expatriated in the main to France to develop their expertise and make contacts (on three year contracts, renewable for three years) – the top UK posts are filled by these people. An expatriate position also enables employees to bring technical expertise back into the UK. In France, employees may be expatriated into the UK or the US, usually for five years, as part of their development for top jobs such as that of general manager.

Skills gaps and transfer of expertise

Expatriation may be required for project work. This is the case, for example, at Hogan Systems where it is the expatriate's job to install and launch new software systems and to train local employees to run the system themselves. This usually takes two years.

At Westland, employees are expatriated for the specific expertise necessary to complete a particular job (with teams of specialists and support staff on three month or longer postings) and manage projects (with such management postings being for a year or more).

At Digital, project managers may be transferred to another location for the duration of a project, usually up to three years, or to specialize in certain techniques and to bring those skills back to the home location. Employees may be expatriated for career development reasons especially at senior level. Business managers, for example, are likely to be expatriated to develop their career aspirations and talents and also to spread their knowledge. Postings are usually for two to five years, although such assignments occasionally may prove to be permanent.

Developing new teams
On acquiring European companies, depending on the quality of the management team, a company may need to expatriate UK management personnel to direct the new operation or to train local staff in the company's procedures. As part of its programme of acquisition of small generic drug manufacturers, it is Rhône-Poulenc's French HQ's policy to place one of its financial controllers into the new company. And at Grand Metropolitan, a new management team is sent in after an acquisition if the need arises.

Recruitment and selection

The recruitment and selection of expatriates is an area which is attracting increasing attention. For example, at Tioxide, expatriation is part of the company's strategy for succession planning – it is used to develop a 'pool of competence'. Under Grand Metropolitan's succession planning process, international successors for existing staff are considered on merit and cross country moves are not unusual. International assignments are increasingly used in individuals' development programmes as the company builds a cadre of internationally mobile executives.

The recruitment of potential expatriates tends to fall into two main categories: young, new graduates are hired by companies with the 'we grow our own' philosophy; and experienced, skilled personnel who may be taken on at senior levels to fill skills gaps or to provide specialist expertise. The recruitment and selection process for expatriates involves identifying both technical competence and cultural flexibility. In some companies professional qualifications are seen as crucial; in others experience is more important. A European business education and experience may also be considered important.

Companies such as Hogan Systems and Westland Helicopters which are exporting project teams require technical competence in their expatriates, although some cultural flexibility is necessary if they are to settle in and operate effectively. Employees working overseas in a managerial capacity or in a sales role must be able to adapt and work well within the culture of their host country. The requirement for professional qualifications and/or a European business education is not considered important by the majority of companies. However, this might be the result of the British preference for experience and technical competence. For example, in Rhône-Poulenc, the French HQ is keen to attract employees with business qualifications as well as technical knowledge. In the UK HQ of the company, however, there is less emphasis on qualifications: employees and potential recruits are judged on performance and experience.

When recruiting new graduates and buying in skills at a more senior level, companies such as BP look for more than just good degrees and technical skills from their potential international and European executives. Besides being able to fit in with company values, these people must have 'something extra' – they need to be able to meet 'world-wide criteria'. Graduate recruitment at BP is being extended to countries outside the home location. However, in the short term, the hiring of employees throughout Europe will be carried out according to UK criteria.

Euro-managers
Many companies are considering recruiting and developing so-called Euro-managers who would work within various European locations. They are looking for multi-lingual and multi-cultural people with, they say, charisma, who can settle down quickly and fit in with the company's ethos. Some, such as Reckitt & Colman, already have a global management pool which already operates within Europe as well as other countries, and have no plans for a separate European cadre of expatriates.

Relocation package

Pay
Expatriates working in Europe would generally expect to receive the local market rate. Surprisingly, the case studies present a more varied picture. Some, such as Willis Faber, base remuneration on the host country's pay policy while maintaining a notional home country salary for pension and repatriation purposes. Others, like Tioxide and Hogan Systems, pay the home country salary plus a supplement (usually 15 per cent) for working abroad. Expatriates at Digital receive a pay package which ensures that they are neither

better nor worse off. To add to the range of practice on pay some organizations, for instance Reckitt & Colman, maintain expatriates' net disposable income and add an overseas premium.

It is difficult to predict what is likely to happen to pay after the arrival of the Single European Market. One company believes that there would be a trend towards the levelling up of European pay, with a greater emphasis on cash because of its greater visibility in competitive labour situations. By contrast, another employer believes that no change is likely after 1992; that labour markets are unlikely to reach equilibrium for some years, perhaps even for two generations. However, it is likely that increasing premiums will will be paid for international managers who are multi-lingual and have multi-cultural experience.

Benefits
Most organizations believe that there will be a reduction in the number of tax effective benefits across countries and, indeed, changes are already taking place. To begin with, there appears to be a trend towards the provision of company accommodation, rather than a housing allowance. (This has tax advantages and removes the burden of househunting.) The company car is an emotive issue and so in countries where it is unusual for anyone other than directors to have company cars, employers are providing financial compensation for the loss of the vehicle. Indeed, employers are increasingly recognizing that countries cannot export their own benefit systems and impose their own standards on another country regardless of whether their own benefits fit in with a different culture.

On items such as leave there are also likely to be changes. Domestic relocation policies usually allow weekend travel home if an employee is separated from his or her family. International relocation policies tend to allow home leave only once a year. Europe is so close to the UK that employees can travel home regularly.

It is currently BP's policy to treat expatriates in, say, Australia, in a similar manner to those in Europe – they receive the same number of leave passages. BP is now rethinking its allowances policy, as it believes that there should be differently structured packages for relocations between and within continents. Overall, companies seem not to be standardizing benefits worldwide.

Training

By contrast, however, companies are becoming more international in their outlook towards training. They now emphasize language training, cultural awareness training, foreign country briefing and management development. More and more they also involve spouses and children in these types of training.

Westland Helicopters began language training for specific assignments in 1988. The company was to expatriate a team to Italy and so language tuition was provided in-company for employees and spouses. Now French, German and Italian classes are run in the evenings at three levels: beginners, intermediate and advanced. At Rhône-Poulenc, the two official languages of the group are English and French and expatriates are expected to understand both. Training is provided in-company or the company pays for employees to attend evening classes. Intensive language training by Berlitz is used by Reckitt & Colman and BP. Hogan Systems encourages expatriates to teach themselves by using training tapes paid for by the company.

Foreign country briefing for Europe is also beginning to be provided. In the past, companies considered that, as Europe is so close and as most employees have already visited the country concerned, briefing was unnecessary but now they are recognizing the importance of briefing to help employees and their families to settle in.

At Westland Helicopters, for example, when appropriate, the overseas assignments manager visits company project locations overseas, collects maps, literature, shop prices, etc. and provides in-company briefing to potential expatriates. Data from external consultancies is also given. 'Open door' policies are also common: for example, French expatriates at Rhône-Poulenc who relocate to the UK receive a pack of data, assistance with finding accommodation and an 'open door' to the personnel department.

Cultural awareness training for expatriates going to Europe is not common at present, although companies are now considering sending expatriates and their spouses on intensive courses such as those offered by the Centre For International Briefing. The main obstacles here seem to be difficulty in finding the time for employees to attend and, indeed, overcoming employee resistance to the training. Some companies offer in-house cultural awareness training but find that employees do not take it up. The reason for this could be that as we are so close to Europe we all believe we understand the cultures there anyway.

Management development training, specifically geared to working in Europe and/or internationally is also becoming more
widespread. Grand Metropolitan runs a two day international
awareness management training programme in an international
location (e.g. Paris) to provide greater insight into cultural differences and perspectives. The participants must work on and
complete a project on the spot which forces them to operate in
the foreign culture.

The remainder of this chapter contains nine case studies which
demonstrate how various organizations are adapting their policies
and procedures in the light of the Single European Market.

Case studies

Tioxide UK Ltd

Background
Tioxide is a multi-national company with operations world-wide
although the largest sector of its business is in Europe. It is
the leading manufacturer of titanium pigments in Europe. The
company is about to build a new plant on the East coast of
Malaysia. Other company sites include Durban in South Africa,
Tasmania and Quebec in Canada. The company has seven manufacturing plants of which five are in Europe. Of these, two are in
the UK at Teesside and Grimsby. The others are in Huelva in
South West Spain, Scarlino in Italy and Calais in France.

Tioxide plans to expand its operations in Germany by enlarging
its sales organizations. This will be spearheaded from the French
centre. It has already increased operations on the ground in
Europe (for example the Italian plant resulted from an acquisition
five years ago) and plans to continue to develop the European
sites.

Group manager for Europe – 1992
From March 1989, a new post was created by Tioxide. The 'group
manager for Europe – 1992' has the function of making Tioxide
aware of the implications of the Single European Market. This
job involves promoting awareness at operational and strategic
levels. Operational details include safety procedures, labelling
products, gaining clearances for new acquisitions/mergers, etc. At

the strategic level, the job consists of exploring the opportunities from relocating sites within Europe.

The manager has a team consisting of 10 senior managers of different nationalities from different functions in Spain, France, Italy and the UK. Their role is to analyse their own company positions and to make group level recommendations about proposed changes with the aim of creating a general European strategy.

Numbers
The company has around 30 expatriates at present, although the number is likely to rise to between 40 and 50 with the construction of the Malaysian plant. The majority of them are Europeans and around 20 are currently employed in the company's European locations.

Reasons for expatriation
Employees are asked to relocate abroad for management development purposes, i.e. to widen their experience of international management, and because they are needed for a specific job. Secondments generally last between one and three years. At production manager level, a three year secondment is required to assimilate information and to be able to use it effectively. Expatriation is also used to fill skills gaps and to transfer expertise. For example, there is much movement into and out of the UK for this reason.

An employee from the company's data processing centre in Spain, for example, would work in the company's London centre for training and development purposes and would then return to Spain, taking back knowledge of the London system so that it may be developed there.

Expatriation is part of the company's strategy for succession planning. It is used to develop a 'pool of competence'. Expatriates are used until local managers are developed to the required company standard. This may mean a succession of expatriate assignments for as long as it takes for a local employee to be ready to take charge of the operation.

Recruitment and selection
Tioxide has recently begun to develop a European and global recruitment programme. The graduate milkround will be run in Europe from the summer of 1990 and the company plans to recruit

in countries such as Japan and send recruits to the company's plants and offices worldwide. It is the company's policy to 'grow its own' talent rather than recruit people into senior positions, with the exception of specialist occupations such as legal and accounting functions.

When recruiting, Tioxide seeks good initial qualifications from, for example, chemists and chemical engineers and would expect these people to be members of their own professional institutions. Professional qualifications are considered secondary to graduates' general educational track record.

To be considered suitable for a mobile expatriate career, Tioxide looks for the qualities of leadership and flexibility, a risk-taking approach, the ability to manage people and linguistic skills.

Pay

Secondees receive their home country salary plus a 15 per cent disturbance allowance. In some countries, cost of living is also built in. Furnished accommodation and a car are provided, and employees remain in the home country pension scheme. It is usual for expatriates to move from the home country to the host country and then return to the home country. However, some employees relocate between host countries. Employees with successive secondments remain in the home country pension fund, although the company has an offshore pension fund to make up any deficiencies. Permanent transferees are employed on local salaries and conditions.

Salary levels differ considerably across Europe. These differences need to be overcome if recruitment practices are to operate Europe-wide. For example, if the company recruits a German chemical engineer to work in the UK, a salary higher than that generally paid in Britain would be needed to attract that individual. This could lead either to a raising of pay levels in the UK, or such expatriates only working for the company for a short while. Although the company already uses Hay management consultancy to compare job sizes, it believes that a Europe-wide pay system will need to be devised to promote mobility.

Training

Language training is offered in all the company's European locations. In the UK, French, Spanish and Italian classes are run. In Italy and Spain, English classes are offered. These are attended by company personnel of all levels of seniority and language ability. The sessions last for two hours from 4pm to 6pm so that employees take one hour of company time and use one hour of their own time. Currently the classes are not targetted at particular skills needs, neither are they aimed at specific levels of ability.

Tioxide does not provide cultural awareness training for employees expatriated to Europe. It is usual, however, for employees to have already had contact with colleagues and to have visited the location.

Family
A familiarization trip is offered for the employee and spouse. Dual careers are becoming a feature of expatriate relocation and the company appointed a family's administrator from the beginning of 1989 to look after the family aspects of relocation. The role involves assisting spouses remaining in the home country while employees are abroad either on secondment or on business trips. It also involves finding accommodation for employees relocating into the UK.

The UK personnel department guides the actions of the European personnel departments in finding accommodation for UK-based executives relocating abroad.

Repatriation
Expatriates are subject to careful selection decisions before their secondments. Expatriation is usually part of a succession plan, identified during annual appraisals. As a result, repatriation usually involves promotion but, if not, a job is given of a similar level to that which the expatriate held before the secondment.

Digital Equipment Company

Background
Digital has 15 sites within the UK. It is an American company and is covered by the US Government's export compliance legislation. As such the level of business carried out within certain countries is controlled by licence.

Numbers
In the UK, Digital employs around 160 expatriates: 100 of these have relocated from the UK to overseas locations and 60 are foreign nationals working in the UK.

Digital employs expatriates worldwide. For example, the US, France and Switzerland are the main areas where UK expatriates are employed. (The company's European headquarters is based in Geneva.) Digital has operations in all the European countries. The foreign nationals working in the UK are mainly from the US.

Reasons for expatriation

Employees are expatriated for a number of reasons. Digital's business is that of fast moving technology, so transfer of technological expertise is crucial. For instance, project managers are typically transferred to other company locations for the duration of a project – usually up to three years – to specialize in certain techniques and to bring those skills back to the home location.

Employees may be relocated for career development reasons, especially at senior level. Business managers, for example, may be moved to develop their career aspirations and talents. The duration of the posting is usually between one and five years, although in some instances such assignments may prove to be permanent.

Digital may recruit foreign nationals directly into the company, although the numbers are low: they would be hired generally to fill a particular skills gap.

It may be the case, occasionally, for personnel to be expatriated where there is a mismatch of work and skills, for example when one location has considerable volumes of work but too few skilled people or where the opposite is true and there are too many people in a location with too little work. The company recognizes, however, that it is impractical to relocate large numbers of people, normally only single individuals are sent on assignments. Movement of personnel may also take place when the market changes and it becomes economically advantageous for Digital to operate in particular countries. The relocation of staff internationally may prove preferable to hiring recruits locally, particularly where there is a short term need such as start up and training. The company also benefits from the cross-cultural exchange and wider visibility of its operations.

Recruitment and selection

Digital seeks both technical competence and functional experience within and between units from its expatriate workforce. A degree of cultural flexibility is also required so that the employee is able to live happily in the country and do business with its nationals.

For example, a high level of cultural flexibility is required for a sales executive but this may be less necessary for a hardware engineer. Sales personnel are expected to operate effectively within the host country's culture and so it is often preferable to use locals as salespeople rather than foreign nationals.

Digital is more concerned that employees have a good track record within the company than about their professional qualifications. The Euro-managers of the future are expected to be fluent in English which is the recognized company language as well as that of the country in which they are working.

Pay

For assignments of one to five years, expatriates receive a pay package that ensures that they are neither better nor worse off. This may mean being paid in either the home or the host country depending on conditions in each country (e.g. National Insurance and tax). Pay reviews are given in line with performance and in accordance with either host or home country salary basis. A notional salary is kept for pension and repatriation purposes. Tax advice is offered from an outside firm of chartered accountants: Digital operates a policy of tax equalization.

For permanent international transfers (i.e. assignments for longer than five years or for expatriates who have no intention of returning), employees receive the host country pay and conditions package.

Training

Language lessons are given to assignees during their first 18 months overseas. Training in English is offered to foreign nationals working in the UK. Expatriates relocating from Britain overseas receive language tuition abroad which is administered by the host country.

Family

Digital provides familiarization visits of up to seven days for the spouse and family. After acceptance of the expatriation, the employee and spouse are offered seven days' househunting.

Repatriation

It is Digital's policy that two people hold responsibility for each employee's career, the employee and a sponsor – his or her home country career manager. This is generally a very senior employee, usually someone on, or directly reporting to, a memer of the board of management. This sponsor has a stated commitment to the repatriation and is responsible for ensuring that a suitable job is available for the expatriate on return. Sponsorship relies on the personal commitment of the sponsor to the expatriate; if the sponsor moves on, for example to a foreign assignment, the onus is on the sponsor's replacement to take over the sponsor's role or to ensure an appropriate person does so.

The majority of assignees return to their home country after their assignment but a proportion do transfer to become permanent employees of the host country (especially in the US and Valbonne, France). Also a small number go on to take up a new assignment in another country.

Hogan Systems

Background
Hogan Systems employs some 400 people world-wide. It is an American company and employs 290 people in Dallas and 50 people in New York. Subsidiaries employ 50 people in the UK and 10 in Australia. The company specializes in computer software for the banking, insurance and finance sector and seeks to expand internationally.

Hogan Systems' business is customer-led. The company has carried out a market study into Europe to examine where IBM-based companies are located. The top three places where Hogan Systems will concentrate its business efforts are Germany, Italy and Scandinavia.

A project team has already completed assignments in Portugal and Holland and consultants have undertaken an evaluation exercise in Belgium and Italy. The project teams have included UK consultants and expatriates from Dallas.

Numbers
The number of expatriates depends on the level of project work being carried out: generally, there are about three European projects at any one time, each one employing two to 10 expatriates. It is anticipated that the number of expatriates in Europe will rise considerably. Currently there are 10 in Europe but by 1992, the company envisages that there will be 40.

Reasons for expatriation
It is the expatriates' job to install and launch the new software
system and to train local employees to run the system themselves.
This usually takes around two years. Sales people from the UK
would also be moved around to develop new business.

Recruitment and selection
Hogan Systems anticipates its requirements for personnel to carry
out project work and recruits in the UK or transfers personnel
from Dallas. The company requires technical competence and
knowledge of the IBM mainframe system and/or knowledge of the
financial services sector. Software experience related to bank card
processing systems or credit cards is also considered important.
Professional qualifications are not essential but experience of
working in the financial services sector is.

Technical competence is considered to be crucial for project
work, more so than cultural flexibility. However, salespeople need
to have a high degree of cultural awareness, to have selling
experience in the financial services sector and, preferably, to speak
the host country's language.

As part of the company's mission is to expand internationally,
it is considered important to appoint a Euro-manager. This person
should be multi-lingual and have experience in dealing with several
European countries.

Pay
Typically, an expatriate assignment lasts from between six months
to two years. In these cases, employees remain on the home
country payroll for salary review and benefits purposes but are
considered as local employees for reporting arrangements. Expatriates receive their home country salaries plus 15 per cent.

They also receive tax equalization payments and tax preparation
assistance is given. Employees remain in the home country social
security system for up to two years.

Employees who are on assignments of less than six months
receive travel and subsistence payments, not the full relocation
policy. Employees on assignment for over two years are considered
to be on permanent transfer.

In more expensive countries such as Norway, Hogan Systems is
likely to give expatriates a meal allowance, which is normally only
given to those on short assignments, in addition to the 15 per cent

overseas allowance. An alternative is to increase the percentage amount given.

Training
The company encourages salespeople to learn foreign languages and they are provided with tapes at company expense. The company is now considering sending key personnel to a London-based language school for intensive training. These courses last for 15 days and cost around £9,000 – they might be used for Euro-managers.

Family
The company provides assistance with the cost of accommodation in the overseas location and pays school fees so that children may attend an English speaking school. Language training is not paid for spouses or children. In the company's experience, employees are generally very family orientated and do not wish to uproot their dependants. As a result, Hogan Systems encourages the relocation of single personnel where possible. If employees are married, the company encourages them to take their spouse abroad, rather than leave the spouse in the home country.

Repatriation
Hogan Systems does not have a formal sponsor system but it regards its employees as being extremely valuable and their skills are always in short supply. As a result, expatriates always have a suitable job to which to return.

The company encourages its employees to be flexible and to move to wherever they are needed. Employees may, therefore, either return to their home country after an expatriate assignment or be transferred to another host country.

British Petroleum

Background
British Petroleum is a major world-wide oil company. Tradition-ally, operations have been administered from the UK but in recent years the company has set up two major centres within Europe for the administration of all European operations. A centre in Paris administers the Atlantic seaboard countries, while a German centre covers other European, non-Warsaw pact, BP operations.

The company believes that forming these supra-regional centres within Europe creates efficiency, for example, they reduce duplication of activity. The approach of 1992 has not been the catalyst for this development, although BP has found that the climate associated with 1992 has aided rationalization.

Numbers
BP employs 1,500 expatriates world-wide of whom 1,200 are British. The company expects that this figure will change and that there will be fewer British expatriates, about 800 to 900, and more from other nationalities. In the main, expatriation is to BP's oil companies, rather than to its nutrition subsidiaries.

Currently, there are expatriates in 14 European countries, ranging from one in Austria and Cyprus to 200 in Norway. The majority of expatriates are involved in marketing. It is expected that the number of expatriates working in Switzerland will fall from 30 to around four or five although the total number of people working in Europe will increase.

The numbers of expatriates in Europe who are working in a country outside of their home country base range from one in Spain and in Portugal to 40 in France. It is expected that movement between European countries will increase and there will also be increased movement out of Europe to other continents.

Reasons for expatriation
The main reason for expatriation is for general development, although some employees are moved to fill skills gaps and to transfer expertise. During this process, the company is able to 'cream off' the fast tracking employees for further development.

Recruitment and selection
BP recruits graduates and then trains and promotes from within. Some intake is necessary higher up the hierarchy, although the emphasis is on the company growing its own. Each company in Europe recruits to meet its own needs. However, some of the European locations are extending their graduate recruitment into countries other than the home location. In the short term, hiring of employees will be according to UK criteria. The philosophy is to achieve group ownership of these recruits so that they can be relocated and accepted by the receiving country without the host location considering their assignment imposed. However, the company recognizes that it has yet to be determined whether

recruiting European graduates according to UK selection criteria and values will prove suitable.

In its graduate recruitment programme, BP looks for employees who fit in with company values. Some 60 per cent of the graduate intake are engineers and so technical skills are required. Although the company expects recruits to have a good qualification, they need not have first class honours degrees. Instead, BP looks for 'something extra'; graduates must be able to meet 'world-wide criteria' as BP hires employees for all parts of the world.

If BP has to buy in skills at a more senior level, the recruitment process aims to identify someone with potential: employees are recruited not into a job, but into a development plan.

Pay

The expatriate pay and benefits policy applies world-wide and its philosophy is to maintain the employee's net disposable income. Added to this is a premium of between 10 and 15 per cent of base salary for expatriation. The premium paid varies with seniority – the more senior the person, the lower the incentive paid.

Expatriates are able to maintain their home based commitments. The company provides free housing in the host country together with educational support and repatriation costs. Employees remain in the home country pension scheme.

Expatriates in, say, Australia are treated in a similar manner to those in Europe, receiving, for example, the same number of leave passages. The company is rethinking its allowances policy, believing that there should be a differently structured package for moves between continents. The policy needs to reflect the differences between outward and return expatriation and that of successive host country postings.

Training

English is the business language used by BP. The company trains all employees who have to operate in English. Training is also given in the language of the foreign country to which they are expatriated if this is necessary, using Berlitz language courses. The company is considering introducing briefing for European transfers.

Management development courses, addressing such issues as world-wide marketing strategies, are held in Britain. Expatriates come to the UK from different countries, cultures and businesses for training.

Family

The company uses the Berlitz language courses for employees and their spouses, although no language tuition is provided for children. Some briefing is provided for spouses, although this is, in the main, job related. However, BP is beginning to build up data-banks of information on living in overseas countries and to introduce networking with expatriates already in the host location. In this way, the employee and spouse gain an understanding of the new location. Reconnaisance visits are also offered before the expatriate agrees to the assignment.

Repatriation

BP has a career development system through which the individual is 'tracked' and his or her career examined by a functional management employee. In BP Chemicals, there is a sponsor scheme in operation. Under this system, the person who is responsible for the employee begins the repatriation process one year before the expatriate is due to return by analysing and taking responsibility for their reabsorption back into the UK division.

For employees involved in exploration, there is a 'godfather' system. Under this, the functional manager for the petroleum engineers is a resource manager and he or she acts as a broker between the individual and the next receiving line centre.

In the main, expatriates return from the host country to the home country, although there are currently around 40 to 50 expatriates per year who relocate between host countries in Europe.

Rhône-Poulenc Ltd

Background

Rhône-Poulenc is a French pharmaceutical company with major facilities in every European country. It has production sites in the UK, Germany, Italy, Spain and Switzerland and 40 factories in France. There are small facilities in many other European countries and operations throughout the Far East, Middle East, Australasia, Africa, North and South America.

The Single European Market is resulting in increased competition for Rhône-Poulenc, especially from generic manufacturers. The company is beginning to acquire small generic drug companies to cope with this competition and to respond to the market trend towards the use of generics.

Numbers

In 1987, Rhône-Poulenc employed 350 international managers world-wide and by 1990, this number is forecast to increase to 500. Currently, the company has 12 British expatriates working in France and about 20 French expatriates working in the UK. There are a few other transfers between European countries, for example one expatriate from Eire is now working in Britain. Rhône-Poulenc forecasts that numbers of expatriates in Europe will rise as the company's operations become more closely integrated.

Reasons for expatriation

British employees are usually expatriated to France to develop their expertise (and bring it back) and to make contacts. The top UK posts are filled by people who have had an expatriate posting to France. In France, employees may be expatriated into the UK or the US as part of their development for top jobs such as that of general manager.

Relocation from the UK to other countries is less common, although if this did happen, the expatriation would be controlled and administered from Paris.

French expatriates working in the UK do so on a five year assignment; British expatriates working in France are on three year assignments (this is for social security reasons). The British assignments to France are renewable for a further three years if both parties agree.

As part of its programme of acquisition of small generic drug manufacturers, it is the French headquarters' policy to place one of its financial controllers into the new company. By contrast, the UK arm of the firm would evaluate whether the acquired company's top management understands Rhône-Poulenc's demands and, if not, would install a new managing director from the UK. The rationale behind the decision is to ensure that the top person in the newly acquired company is able to undertake any rationalization necessary – for example by moving production to where facilities are cheaper.

Recruitment and selection

Rhône-Poulenc in France is keen to attract employees with business qualifications as well as technical knowledge. The top company employees have been educated at the leading business schools in France. The company believes that, with good quality qualifications and background, these executives will be suitable for many different positions within the company.

In the UK, however, there is less emphasis on attracting staff with business qualifications. Employees and potential recruits are judged on performance and experience.

Personnel recruited into the British, French and other European companies usually come from their home countries and this is unlikely to change. For example, the company does not expect its German operations to recruit from other countries directly although it accepts that a labour flow from low-paying countries such as Greece into high paying ones like Germany may occur. However, cultural and language differences are likely to slow any such process down.

Currently, under the parent company's initiative there is a group wide effort to recruit 25 year old managers. The company wants good, young, bright, international graduates with the appropriate technical qualifications and MBAs, or graduates from French or American business schools. They are to be recruited on a contract in which they agree to work in two countries other than their own. Existing employees are also to be considered for this pool of 30 to 40 international personnel. So far about 15 employees have been recruited to this elite group and the company plans to recruit the same number each year for three or four years. If there are no drop-outs, the total will reach 60, although it is expected that some will leave, resulting in a total of about 40.

The pool will contain truly international managers who will work mainly in Europe and the USA and other developed OECD countries, although they may undergo one expatriate posting to a third world nation. The group is expected to become as capable as the company's senior management team and to have outstanding abilities. They are required to have full cultural flexibility, an international outlook and the ability to think globally. The company expects that it will take between 10 and 15 years before the group will affect company strategy.

Pay

Expatriates receive the local salary paid by the host country plus an expatriate premium of between 10 and 60 per cent, paid by the home country. In Europe, the expatriate premium or hardship allowance is generally 10 per cent, although in some countries as much as 20 per cent of salary may be paid. If the home country's salary levels are such that the expatriate's spending power at home is greater than the local salary, then a supplement is paid in the home country. A transfer allowance of half a month's salary plus 10 per cent per child in care is also paid.

A notional salary is maintained in the home country. This is used for assessing the employee's pension and is paid to the employee on repatriation.

Employees remain in the home country pension fund whenever possible. UK personnel relocating to France receive a written guarantee that their UK and French pension benefits will be added together and that, if this sum provides a lower pension than would have been achieved through continuous service in the UK, the company (not the pension fund) makes up the difference.

Benefit conditions differ between countries: in France, for instance, few employees (other than board directors) receive cars. If a UK expatriate gives up a company car on secondment to France, the value of that car is included in the benefit package.

Rhône-Poulenc also gives some assistance with housing. Expatriates are expected to pay 10 per cent of their salaries towards housing costs, with any additional expenditure met by the company.

If an expatriate completes two three-year assignments in France and elects to stay on a permanent transfer basis, the company alters the pay and benefits package over a four year transitional period by tapering the home country benefits in three equal instalments. In the fourth year, housing benefit is also taken away, leaving the permanent transferee on local salary and conditions.

The company plans to maintain its current system of pay and benefits after 1992, believing that labour markets are unlikely to reach equilibrium for many years.

Training

The official languages of the group are English and French and expatriates are expected to understand these languages. If they are working in a country where English or French are not the main languages, the company pays for language training to a social level – they are not expected to speak it to a business level, instead a translator would be provided if necessary. To reach a social level in the new language, the company pays for 50 hours of training which is usually given before departure.

In the UK, the company encourages employees of all levels to learn French and Rhône-Poulenc pays for French lessons in-company or for employees to attend evening classes. Classes run in-company are on three levels – basic, intermediate and advanced. For managers, the company pays for individual French tuition. Tutors are employed to visit the company's three biggest sites and provide French tuition on a one to one basis. Discussion groups of three managers led by the tutor are also held for those with an advanced grasp of the language.

Employees expatriated to Europe receive briefing materials published by Employment Conditions Abroad Ltd. If employees request cultural awareness training, they may be able to attend the Centre For International Briefing. The receiving company's staff are expected to provide support, for example, French expatriates relocating into the UK receive a pack of data, assistance with finding accommodation and an 'open door' to the personnel department.

Management training courses are run in Britain and France, for managers based in the overseas location as well as expatriates. For example, in the UK incoming French managers and French expatriates may receive training in negotiating skills, take part in video training work, practise English and have discussions with home country based managers employed in similar jobs. The aim of the one week UK-based course (and two week French-based course) is for managers to improve their language, their contacts and to absorb the local culture.

Family
The company pays for 50 hours of language training for the spouse and children may also receive language training, depending on their age. The family receives a pack of information on the new location. Spouses are not sent on cultural awareness courses but the company does pay for the employee and spouse to visit the country before the assignment.

Dual careers are causing some problems to the company but not as many as might be expected. The company culture is such that employees need to undergo expatriate assignments in France to progress in their careers. Employees can apply for these expatriate positions or they may be approached. Through the use of a career development form and interview, the company can assess candidates' career aspirations and the extent to which these can be achieved, taking into account the career plans of the employees' spouses.

In France, dual careers do not present a problem to the movement of expatriates.

Repatriation
Responsibility for repatriation is at divisional rather than an individual level. A regularly updated list records where expatriates are, which location is paying for them and which location has responsibility for their return. Six to nine months before an expatriate's due date for repatriation, the computerized list records their impending return and the division is responsible for identifying vacancies which will make use of their new experience. The computerized system effectively operates as a world-wide central clearing house. If the employees cannot be given a suitable post at the home base, they may be offered another job elsewhere.

Younger, junior staff usually return from an expatriate assignment to a promotion. More senior people are usually transferred abroad and receive promotion in the new post, returning to a job of a similar level to that held abroad but with a view to promotion when a suitable vacancy occurs. If the expatriate has to return to a lower graded job because no other suitable vacancy arises, their notional salary is maintained for three years.

British expatriates working in an overseas location outside Europe are likely to be relocated from one host country to another; those working in Europe are more likely to return to Britain. French expatriates working in Britain are also likely to return to their home base. Rhône-Poulenc in France generally does not relocate expatriates on a permanent basis: career paths are most likely to involve an expatriation, followed by a return to the home base, and then a further expatriation, again followed by return home.

Willis Faber Plc

Background
Willis Faber employs 5,430 people in the UK and 1,000 people overseas. The company specializes in international insurance and re-insurance broking, as well as offering an underwriting

management service to UK and overseas insurance companies, and has offices worldwide. The company's European offices are in London, Paris and Brussels and there are offices in Madrid, Lisbon, Oporto, Milan as well as in West Germany, Greece and Switzerland, and shortly in Denmark. Outside Europe, the company has offices in North and South America, Australasia, Africa, the Near and Far East. About 60 per cent of its business is traded in currencies other than sterling.

The company has recently acquired 20 per cent of a local direct broker in Belgium. This action is specifically geared to the approach of the Single European Market in 1992 with the aim of increasing the company's presence on the ground in Europe.

Following the successful installation of a DEC computer network linking a number of French companies with its own system, the company plans to extend the DEC network to other continental countries during the 1990s.

Numbers

The company employs around 30 expatriates world-wide, two of whom are women. There is at the moment one British expatriate in Paris and one in Brussels. There are also two British expatriates on longer-term assignments in Portugal and an Italian on assignment in the UK. The number of expatriates is increasing.

Reasons for expatriation

Non-UK staff require knowledge and experience of the Lloyds London insurance/re-insurance market and so both senior and junior employees in France and Belgium are relocated from their Paris and Brussels offices into the UK to gain experience and transfer their expertise back to their home countries. The head of the Italian office is also currently working in London. The other European offices are staffed by local people and although the company has considered expatriating staff for development purposes this has not occurred yet.

Employees are not promoted on expatriation from Britain but usually receive promotion on their return. Generally, European expatriates working in London do so for four to five years. British expatriates working in the Paris and Brussels offices are usually assigned there for two or three years, occasionally longer.

The company has two schools of thought on expatriation to Europe. First, because Europe is close, it should be serviced by business trips instead of an expatriate assignment. The alternative view is that the company should show a UK presence in overseas locations. As the company acquires direct brokers in Europe, its need for UK specialists experienced in the London market to work in Europe is likely to grow.

Recruitment and selection
General recruitment is carried out by the local company office, although the London headquarters recruits managers or key personnel for all locations. The London insurance and re-insurance market is unique and it is essential that senior staff employed in Europe know it. The company, therefore, seeks to recruit Europeans who will come to London for training or to appoint British people who speak another European language to train in the UK and then work elsewhere in Europe.

In the short to medium term, it is likely that British recruits willing to work in other parts of Europe will form the main source of supply. Willis Faber seeks technical competence and fluency in a European language other than English. Because the insurance and re-insurance environment is so specialized, Europe-wide business experience is not sought.

The company prefers to recruit and train single people in their late 20s, as they are generally mobile and willing to be trained in the company's business and methods. The company recruits around 10 to 20 graduates in the UK each year. Graduates in economics, law, mathematics and languages are considered to have suitable academic backgrounds. The company is currently conducting a language survey of its divisions to identify employees with language abilities. These people may prove to be candidates for expatriation to Europe.

As it develops its direct broking business in Europe, Willis Faber may recruit more retail-based insurance personnel, rather than those with re-insurance knowledge of the wholesale insurance market.

The company is considering establishing a pool of European managers to be based within Europe and available for transfer between European countries. They would be expected to be good linguists, be able to settle quickly into a new cultural environment, fit in with the company's ethos and, says the company, possess charisma. The company anticipates problems, however, in determining notional salaries, pension contributions, etc., although clearly such decisions would have to be taken and agreed before the European assignment.

Pay

Expatriates receive local salaries which are slightly enhanced by the payment of a housing allowance, and they are covered by the home country medical insurance scheme. British employees are encouraged to remain in the UK social security system and the company maintains their non-contributory pension scheme contributions in the home country. Expatriates in France and Belgium also receive company contributions into the French social security system.

A notional salary is maintained at home which is kept in line with salaries paid to peers and pension contributions in the home country are based on this. When employees return after the assignment they usually receive more than this notional figure as a result of promotion.

Cost of living differentials are paid where necessary. The company is facing increasing pressure from local nationals in Portugal to raise pay levels as the insurance industry there grows and staff shortages result.

Training

Currently the company has no language training programme although encouragement in developing language skills is envisaged for the future. Briefing by Employment Conditions Abroad Ltd or The Centre For International Briefing is offered but expatriates relocating to Europe rarely accept this. Management conferences are held in London once a year for European managers to discuss issues of concern.

The company mounts a four week insurance course twice a year to which young, overseas based insurance staff are invited to attend to acquire knowledge of the workings of the London market and the company's role in it.

Family

Employees' families accompany them on assignment unless it is a short term trip. Medical benefits apply to families as well as employees. Individuals may put themselves forward for expatriation at their annual appraisal or they may be approached by the company; either way the assignment is discussed with the spouse. If he or she has serious reservations about the posting, the potential expatriate would not be assigned to that location.

Repatriation
The personnel manager responsible for international relocation acts as an 'uncle' to expatriates. At the annual salary review, this manager is responsible for discussions on the expatriate's salary with his or her line managers and six to nine months before repatriation, he or she is responsible for determining a suitable job, title and salary at the home base which reflects the expatriate's new level of skill and expertise.

Reckitt & Colman Plc

Background
The Reckitt & Colman group is a UK-based organization which manufactures and markets branded consumer goods. Its main products are home and personal care items, pharmaceuticals, food, industrial pigments and artists' materials. The company has operations throughout Europe, North and South America, Australasia, the Indian subcontinent, the Far East and Africa. In Europe, the company has operations in every EEC country.

Reckitt & Colman is pursuing a programme of acquisitions and rationalization throughout Europe to explore the increased opportunities offered by the Single European Market. The plans involve the overall simplification and realignment of operations, concentrating on fewer activities to give a greater focus on core product lines. As part of these moves, the UK will manufacture some of the company's most successful European product lines, whilst others will be transferred from the UK to sites around Europe.

For example, Reckitt & Colman has announced that Steradent production will be transferred to Germany where a company that manufactures a similar product, has been bought. It is the company's aim that 'dedicated factory units' producing one product for the whole of Europe 'will lead to higher levels of efficiency, improved product quality and customer services.'

Numbers
The company employs between 40 and 50 expatriates worldwide fewer than half of whom are British. Currently there are 12 expatriates working in the UK (the only continental European being a Belgian) and eight in continental Europe. Of these

eight, there are seven working in six different countries and one Frenchman working in Italy.

Reasons for expatriation
Expatriation is an integral part of the career development process for those employees being trained for the top. When vacancies arise at senior level, the company looks worldwide for individuals with the necessary skills. Expatriation is also used to transfer expertise and to cross-fertilize product knowledge and ideas. Typically an expatriate assignment lasts for three years.

Recruitment and selection
The majority of recruitment is carried out in the local country. Staff who are relocated abroad are those moving to fill skills gaps or for development purposes. Within each unit there is a management development scheme from which employees demonstrating sufficient potential are identified and considered for an international move. Head Office personnel staff visit the major units around the world once a year, the smaller company units once every two years, and spend time with each expatriate. Until recently, experience within the company was expected before consideration was given to an international career. However, the firm is now setting up a scheme to identify bright, young graduates with potential to develop them earlier for an international fast track. Professional qualifications are considered to be important, although technical competence and experience are thought to be more valuable and language abilities are useful. The company has no plans for a separate cadre of European expatriates but will maintain its global pool of expatriate talent.

Pay
Expatriates are paid on the host country salary scales, unless this provides lower purchasing power than they would have enjoyed in the home country, plus a little extra for working overseas. The test is to set a home country notional gross salary for the size of job being done in the host country; deduct notional tax and social security contributions; add a 10 per cent foreign service incentive to give a notional net salary. This is then converted to the host country currency using a purchasing power rate on 70 per cent of it and current exchange rate on the remaining 30 per cent of the notional salary. If the result is greater than the actual host country net salary, an allowance is paid that, after deductions, will make

up the deficit. In addition, a relocation allowance of 15 per cent of gross salary is paid on expatriation and repatriation.

Expatriates remain in the home country pension scheme when possible. British expatriates working in France join the French social security scheme and their occupational scheme contributions are suspended.

Expatriates on assignments of less than 12 months remain on their home country salaries but permanent transferees receive the same pay and conditions as local nationals.

Training
Employees assigned overseas are given intensive language training on a one to one basis by Berlitz. Training is flexible in that it may be given in the evenings or as full days of tuition. Cultural awareness training is not yet offered to expatriates going to Europe although it is likely that it will be in the near future. The company believes that it may be a problem for expatriates to find time to undergo sufficient training while winding down their old jobs, learning a language and preparing for a new assignment. All middle managers going abroad attend a one week marketing strategy course and senior managers attend a two week international management development course.

Family
Language training to the same level of competence as the employee is provided for the spouse but not for children.

Repatriation
The home country issues a repatriation letter that guarantees a position in the home country and sets out the terms of the expatriate's repatriation. In practice, expatriates may find that they are offered a job anywhere in the world.

Westland Helicopters

Background
Westland Helicopters is based in the UK at Yeovil with operations in Weston-super-Mare. Its business in supplying helicopters to the armed forces and overseas markets involves overseas project work. Westland sees the way forward as being through collaborative ventures with European and other partners.

There are two main types of expatriate assignments: three month projects (usually termed extended visits) and one year or longer long-term assignments. Those on all projects are generally employed as technical specialists and support staff as necessary to the project's requirements. In some cases, British specialists work alongside their European counterparts during a collaborative venture. Employees on longer postings fill technical specialist and managerial roles or provide long term back-up to clients. In some countries, Westland employees are seconded to subsidiaries.

Numbers
The company currently employs 48 long term expatriates, i.e. employees on one year or more overseas contracts which may be extended even further, and 26 local nationals. Between January and April 1989, there were 60 expatriates on short-term assignments (three month overseas contracts). Assignments may be to North or South America, Asia or other European countries.

Relocation is mostly from Britain to the host country and back; not between host countries. The numbers of expatriates have increased from around 12 five years ago to the current total of 48.

Reasons for expatriation
Employees are expatriated for their technical expertise necessary to complete and support projects and manage them. The numbers of long-term expatriates and those on extended visits have grown as a result of the company's increased amount of overseas business and collaborative ventures. Customers also expect a greater degree of support to be available on the ground and so major projects often require the setting up of a local in-country product support office.

Recruitment and selection
The company does not recruit personnel for overseas assignments. In-company employees are selected according to the skills, knowledge and experience required to complete the job.

Pay
Employees receive a notional base UK salary which can be adjusted according to the calibre of the overseas work and hours through a temporary job supplement. In addition, they receive a foreign service premium of 10 per cent for Europe (or 15 per cent elsewhere), paid monthly with salary. As an alternative, it may be

possible for employees to receive this premium as an up-front settling-in allowance. A cost of living differential is also paid if applicable. Occasionally, a completion bonus may be given, depending on location. Employees also receive tax equalization and tax advice before departure, while overseas and on return. The company also pays for furnished accommodation and transport. Employees remain in the UK social security scheme if possible and the company pays the employers' UK social security contributions. They also stay in the company pension scheme. Overseas allowances are not pensionable; only the notional salary applies for pension purposes.

Training
Language training is given when necessary. The company has recently expatriated a team to Italy and language tuition was provided in-company for two mornings a week. Employees attended classes for 30 minutes before work and during the first hour of the working day, for two to three months.

The company began language training a year ago for its Italian project and now French, German and Italian classes are run in the evening. Those who require languages for their work gain places on the course; others may attend if there are spare places. Classes are run at three levels: beginners, intermediate and advanced.

Cultural awareness training and briefing has been provided by the Centre For International Briefing for employees and spouses being expatriated to 'difficult' countries, e.g. Korea. As yet, such training has not been given to expatriates going to other European countries. However, the company's overseas assignments manager provides maps, literature, shop prices, etc. to expatriates going to continental Europe. Data from Employment Conditions Abroad Ltd and/or Organization Resources Counselors, Inc. is also used as appropriate. The overseas assignments manager visits some company project locations overseas to provide in-house briefings to employees and answer questions.

Family
The company pays for basic education costs and books for children and provides language training for spouses as appropriate. As part of the preparation for an Italian assignment, spouses were invited to attend a one and a half hour lesson (after employees had had their lesson), on two mornings a week. The company is considering

extending briefing courses to continental European assignments if appropriate. (Briefing has been used as a 'one off' for a Korean assignment.)

Repatriation
Overseas assignments are job-related, so the transfer to and from the UK does not necessarily involve promotion. However, long term overseas postings could, indirectly, improve the long term expatriate's career prospects in the home country. The company gives a contractual commitment that expatriates return to a job in the UK at the same level as they were enjoying before the assignment. The company is planning to use the Hay system to ensure that employees' jobs are evaluated as broadly equal. If the job abroad is more senior than that of their UK post, this is recognized through the temporary job supplement, not through a pay rise, so that when employees return to the UK, they return to their notional salaries.

The overseas assignments manager in conjunction with salary administration, contacts the employee's director and managers several months before the repatriation date is due, so that suitable posts may be identified.

Grand Metropolitan

Grand Metropolitan is a UK company involved in the supply and distribution of food and drink as well as the restaurant and leisure business. The company has recently taken over a number of businesses in Europe, including a restaurant business in Germany and the Greek drinks company, Metaxa. These acquisitions enable the company to gain a greater presence in the market in Europe. The company is also expanding its marketing and distribution network in Europe and, with its takeover of the Pillsbury Company in early 1989, it now has a large US interest.

Grand Metropolitan has set up a main board advisory committee on 1992 issues which has a sub-group examining aspects of personnel. This is examining three key factors: compensation and benefits; training and management development; and employment policy.

Reasons for expatriation
The majority of Grand Metropolitan's expatriate transfers are to and from the USA. However, on acquiring European companies, British or American expatriates may be required to work in the newly acquired company to transfer expertise and develop and train local employees in the company's procedures. If the need arises, a senior management team, usually comprising a finance manager, a personnel manager and a general manager, may head the new operation for up to a three year period. In general, expatriate assignments are for between six months and three years.

Recruitment and selection
Grand Metropolitan seeks both technical competence and cultural flexibility from its expatriates. The company has begun hiring graduate recruits from European business schools to work internationally. Under the succession planning system, international successors for existing staff are considered on merit and cross country moves are not unusual. International assignments are increasingly used in individual's development programmes as the company builds a cadre of internationally mobile exeutives.

Pay
Expatriates working in continental Europe receive either the host or the home country package depending on location. For example, in Germany and France, the host country package applies; in Spain and Portugal, the home country package applies. Where employees do not receive the host country package a cost of living allowance is given.

In considering the implications of 1992 on pay practices, Grand Metropolitan's personnel committee for 1992 considers that the following are likely to affect compensation and benefits practice in Europe:

• a trend towards levelling up of European pay
• greater emphasis on cash conditioned by its greater visibility in competitive labour situations
• a reduction in the number of tax effective benefits across countries
• increasing premiums paid for international managers with a number of languages and multi-cultural experience
• destabilization of some local labour markets, caused by a Europe-wide labour shortage for certain types of staff

- increasing number of international assignees
- transfer of manufacturing facilities to cheaper sources of blue collar labour within Europe which may slow down rates of increase in higher paid countries.

Training
Training is generally the responsibility of each individual company within Grand Metropolitan. For example, language training is organized by individual companies in the group – Grand Met foods has an arrangement with Brunel University to provide a two week intensive 'submersion' course. Language training is generally job orientated but in some divisions, more informal lunchtime or evening language lessons are provided and paid for by the company.

Certain training programmes are run group-wide on an international basis. A five day senior management training programme is run in the UK with the London Business School and a similar programme is run in the US with Columbia University. Between 16 and 20 people attend the course at a time and one third of the course participants are usually from outside the home country. The course tackles strategic issues including marketing, finance, international affairs and organizational change. It is an opportunity for senior managers across the group to meet and exchange ideas.

The company runs a two day international awareness programme in an international location, two or three times a year. This is specifically designed for those employees travelling abroad and/or those with responsibilities overseas. About 16 participants attend each course, which includes training in cultural differences and non-verbal behaviour. Participants have to complete a project during the course which forces them to operate practically and effectively in the country where the programme is held.

Family
'Acclimatization training' at the Centre For International Briefing in the UK or at a similar centre in the US may be offered for the spouse (and children in the US), although such training is usually given for trans-Atlantic relocations, rather than to British families relocating into continental Europe.

Repatriation
The company's relocation policy states that expatriates return to a 'suitable position in the home country subject to prevailing business conditions . . . Full discussion will take place during the

assignment and prior to return with the assignee's nominated career manager'. The nominated career manager is a senior manager, for instance the personnel director of the original employing company or a functional director. If this 'sponsor' leaves the company during the expatriate's assignment, a new career manager is appointed. That person must know the expatriate well and have an interest in him or her returning to a suitable post. Employees are not always guaranteed a post in the same location as they previously worked in the home country and, occasionally, employees are offered further international assignments in other host countries.

7

Lessons from America – the future of relocation in Britain

Labour mobility has always been important but today, in a highly competitive world, it is becoming increasingly necessary. New technology, skills shortages and other factors contribute to this need. If companies are to prosper, compete effectively and maximize performance, they must have the right person in the right place at the right time.

In the USA, the Employee Relocation Council (ERC) was set up in 1964 with 90 corporate members. These were employers who got together to learn from each other and promote more efficient and effective relocation policies and programmes. The US ERC now has a membership of over 10,000, including over 1,200 employers and several thousand relocation service organizations, including relocation management companies, real estate agents and property appraisers.

The success of the Council in the US led to the formation of the Canadian Employee Relocation Council (CERC) in 1982 as Canadian companies recognized the problems associated with relocation and the benefits of having their own centre to provide advice and an information exchange service.

Following on from the success of the American ERC and CERC, the Confederation of British Industry (CBI) surveyed its membership and found that similar demand existed among UK employers for a relocation body to assist companies in moving staff. As a result the CBI Employee Relocation Council (CBI ERC) was launched in April 1986. With a total membership of just under 100 in 1986, membership has now tripled to just under 300 at the end of 1989 – and the numbers of members continue to rise.

The councils have been set up to deal with all aspects of relocation—individual employee domestic and international transfers, group move exercises and the relocation of new recruits.

Relocation is not a static subject – the issues change constantly.

177

With booms and slumps in the housing market, relocation professionals need to be kept up to date on the best way of managing the buying and selling process. Large house price differentials may require innovative action to encourage employees to move.

All three Employee Relocation Councils offer a variety of services to their members. They publish surveys, research reports, newsletters, circulars and directories. All are active in lobbying government on issues of concern to employers relocating staff. Also the councils run a varied programme of workshops, seminars, conferences and exhibitions. An enquiry service is also open to members and all three operate a relocation policy library service for corporate members.

Here in Britain, relocation policies and practice have traditionally tended to lag behind that of our American counterparts. But the situation is changing, fast. In 1986, when the CBI-ERC was launched, the key issue identified by employers was that of the disturbance allowance. What should be paid, to whom and how could employers cope with different tax treatment by tax inspectors? Although this is still of concern to employers, it has long been overtaken by the hazards of the house price divide. (The Americans and Canadians are still trying to thrash out this problem today.) Now, both the Americans and the British are confronted by falling property prices and the problems of selling property in a declining market.

All these difficulties are financial. They cost employers a lot of money. But they all add up to one major headache – resistance to relocation by employees. This reluctance to move can also result from personal and/or social issues and this provides a particular challenge to relocation specialists.

Efforts to encourage employees to move simply through more generous relocation packages are giving way to a more social approach to relocation. For example, in America, compensation paid to spouses for job loss on relocation is rapidly being known as 'the dinosaur' in the relocation package. A more progressive approach, through job search assistance and career counselling for spouses, is seen as the way forward.

US companies are increasingly coming to recognize that they are not just relocating an employee – they are relocating a family. As a result, relocation assistance for children is coming to the fore, with such items as in-company exhibitions aimed at children, relocation games, workbooks and exercises. These are designed to involve youngsters of all ages in the relocation process and are specifically tailored to different age groups. Involvement is now seen as the key to success.

British employers are beginning to consider ways of reducing barriers to relocation raised as a result of family issues. It will not be long before UK employers see the value – and the cost effectiveness – of family involvement in relocation and learn the lessons already understood by successful American companies when moving families both domestically and internationally.

So what is likely to happen next? Mobility throughout Europe is increasing. If established, Employee Relocation Councils in Europe should be able to help European companies in their efforts to move staff, set up new headquarters and move their operations between EC member states.

Relocation is a major issue for Australian employers too. An informal network of service organizations already exists; much research on relocation concerns is being carried out and personnnel journals in Australia are increasingly carrying articles on the subject. Perhaps a body similar to the American, Canadian and British Employee Relocation Councils will be launched there in the not too distant future.

Relocation is a major issue world-wide and its importance for company prosperity can only increase. British companies must keep up to date in their relocation policies and practice if they are to maintain and expand their competitiveness, growth and, ultimately, their profits.

Appendix 1

Regional aid

Under the Regional Initiative, assistance by grant may be available to organizations located in Assisted Areas. There are two forms of assistance – Regional Selective Assistance and the Regional Enterprise Grant. This section outlines the financial help available under these two main schemes and the criteria necessary to qualify. There are many other schemes providing loans and grants to businesses and an outline of those which relate to location decisions is also given.

Regional Selective Assistance
The main form of help available under Regional Selective Assistance (RSA) is in the form of a project grant. The provision of a grant depends on the fixed capital costs of a project and on the number of jobs it is expected to create or safeguard. Grants are negotiable and the amount given is the minimum necessary to enable the project to proceed. It is, therefore, difficult to gain assistance if the project has already begun. It is important to apply for a grant and receive an offer from the Department of Trade and Industry before embarking on the project.

The majority of manufacturing and some service industries are eligible for assistance. Manufacturing industries which are subject to special restrictions by the European Community are ineligible (Currently these are: man-made fibre and yarn; shipbuilding and ship-repair; vehicles; iron and steel; fisheries and certain agricultural products.)

To qualify for assistance five criteria must be met:

- the project must be viable
- assistance must be required so that the project can begin on the basis proposed
- there must be a national or regional benefit (service sector projects serving a local market do not usually qualify)
- the project must either create new jobs or safeguard existing jobs in Assisted Areas
- the finance for the project must come, in the main, from either the proposer's own sources or other private sources.

Project grants may take two forms, either as job related grants or as capital related grants. The Department of Trade and Industry's brochure *The Regional Initiative – Guide To Regional Selective Assistance* states that: 'Job related grants will normally be paid in three equal instalments linked to the creation of jobs and progress with the project. The first instalment is usually paid when one-third of the total jobs linked with the project have been created. For small projects which are completed quickly, the grant may be paid in one or two instalments.' And on capital related grants, it notes: 'Grants related to capital expenditure are normally paid out in instalments related both to your firm's expenditure and progress on the project, including job creation. Eligible costs include purchase of land, site preparation and buildings, and plant and machinery (new or second-hand). Certain non-recurring costs, such as patent rights, professional fees, installation and reinstallation of machinery, may also qualify. The working capital required for a project can be taken into account in fixing grant levels.'

Regional Enterprise Grants

Alternative assistance to RSA is available in the form of a Regional Enterprise Grant but it is not possible to receive both forms of assistance for the same project.

Two grants are available, those for investment projects and those for innovation projects. As with RSA, it is important to apply for assistance before starting the project.

Most manufacturing businesses qualify for assistance, although EC restrictions currently result in the following industries being ineligible: man-made fibre and yarn, isoglucose, shipbuilding and ship repair, iron and steel, fisheries, milk and milk substitutes. Service sector projects which serve only a local market are usually ineligible for an investment grant but they may qualify for an innovation grant. Insurance companies and banks are ineligible for both types.

To qualify, the business or group to which the business is associated must employ fewer than 25 employees (full-time equivalent) worldwide and the project must take place in a Development Area or South Yorkshire.

Grants for investment projects amount to 15 per cent of expenditure on fixed assets in the project, up to a maximum grant of £15,000.

The Department of Trade and Industry notes in its brochure *The Regional Initiative – Application and Guidance Notes for Regional Enterprise Grants* that: 'Eligible costs include plant and machinery (new or second-hand), buildings, purchase of land and site preparation, and vehicles used solely on site'.

Grants for innovation projects 'lead to the development and introduction of new or improved products and processes'. For these 50 per cent of eligible costs up to a maximum grant of £25,000 is paid. The Department of Trade and Industry states: 'All costs up to the point of commercial production may be assisted, including capital costs directly associated with the project. Work can range from feasibility studies, through the development of technical specifications, to the design and manufacture of prototypes. It can be subcontracted where appropriate.'

Other grants and assistance schemes

Loans from Europe and Exchange Risk Cover

The European Investment Bank provides loans to firms in Assisted Areas which are investing in projects which create or safeguard jobs. The loans are for up to half the fixed asset costs of the project.

The European Coal and Steel Community (ECSC) provides loans for projects which create new employment opportunities in coal and steel areas. The loans are for up to half the fixed asset costs of the project. Any manufacturing or service business may qualify.

Exchange Risk Guarantees are available from the ECSC. Loans are made usually in foreign currencies, to be repaid in those currencies but with an exchange risk guarantee ensuring only a sterling liability. All projects assisted must meet RSA criteria and either create new jobs or safeguard existing ones.

Coal, steel and rail areas

British Coal Enterprise Ltd assists in the creation of jobs in coal mining areas by offering assistance (e.g. loans and provision of sites) to businesses setting up, relocating or expanding in coal areas.

British Steel (Industry) aims to generate new employment in steel areas by offering assistance (e.g. loans, share capital, seed capital and contributions towards training) to both manufacturing and service sector firms in 19 'opportunity areas'.

British Rail provides assistance in areas where there have been major BR lay offs or closures. Grants and loans are available but projects must demonstrate job potential.

Urban areas, cities, derelict land and rural areas

The Urban Programme provides funding to local authorities to make assistance available for private sector projects which contribute to the economic development of inner cities.

City grants are aimed at private sector projects to bridge the gap between the estimated cost and estimated value of a project.

Derelict land grants may be payable to compensate for a percentage of the net loss involved in carrying out reclamation work.

The Rural Development Commission provides advice and possibly loans to small firms in rural areas.

Enterprise Zones
The majority of businesses operating in Enterprise Zones benefit from:

- exemption from rates on industrial and commercial property
- exemption from Development Land Tax
- 100 per cent capital allowance for corporation and income tax purposes for capital expenditure on industrial and commercial buildings
- a greatly simplified planning regime
- speedy administration of remaining controls
- reduced requests for statistical information from Government.

Regional aid contact points

Regional Selective Assistance

DTI North-East
Stanegate House
2 Groat Market
Newcastle-upon-Tyne
NE1 1YN
Tel: 091-232 4722

DTI North-West (Manchester)
75 Mosley Street
Manchester M2 3HR
Tel: 061-838 5000

DTI North-West (Liverpool)
Graeme House
Derby Square
Liverpool L2 7UP
Tel: 051-227 4111

DTI Yorkshire and Humberside
Priestley House
3–5 Park Row
Leeds LS1 5LF
Tel: 0532 443171

DTI East Midlands
Severns House
20 Middle Pavement
Nottingham NG1 7DW
Tel: 0602 506181

DTI West Midlands
Ladywood House
Stephenson Street
Birmingham B2 4DT
Tel: 021-632 4111

DTI South-West
The Pithay
Bristol BS1 2PB
Tel: 0272 272666

London
Department of Trade &
Industry
Investment, Development &
Accountancy Services Division
Room 230, Kingsgate House
66–74 Victoria Street
London SW1E 6SW
Tel: 071-215 2565

Scotland: Industry Department for Scotland
Industry Department for
Scotland
Alhambra House
45 Waterloo Street
Glasgow G2 6AT
Tel: 041-248 2855

**Wales: Welsh Office Industry
Department**
Welsh Office
Industry Department
New Crown Building
Cathays Park
Cardiff CF1 3NQ
Tel: 0222 825111

Regional Enterprise Grants

DTI North-East
Stanegate House
2 Groat Market
Newcastle-upon-Tyne
NE1 1YN
Tel: 091-232 4722

DTI North-West
Graeme House
Derby Square
Liverpool
L2 7UP
Tel: 051-224 6300

DTI Yorkshire and Humberside
4th Floor
Fairfax House
Merrion Street
Leeds LS2 8JU
Tel: 0532 338360

DTI East Midlands
Room 15
Spencer House
Spencer Parade
Northampton NN1 5AA
Tel: 0604 21051 Ext. 35

DTI South-West
104 Market Jew Street
Penzance
Cornwall
TR18 3QN
Tel: 0736 60440

London
Department of Trade & Industry
Investment, Development &
Accountancy Services Division
Room 230, Kingsgate House
66–74 Victoria Street
London SW1E 6SW
Tel: 071-215 8459

**Scotland: Industry Department for
Scotland**
Industry Department for
Scotland
Alhambra House
45 Waterloo Street
Glasgow G2 6AT
Tel: 041-248 2855

**Wales: Welsh Office Industry
Department**
Welsh Office
Industry Department
Cathays Park
New Crown Building
Cardiff CF1 3NQ
Tel: 0222 823185

Loans from Europe and Exchange Risk Cover

European Investment Bank
68 Pall Mall
London SW1Y 5ES
Tel: 071-839 3351

European Coal and Steel Community Conversion Loans and Exchange Risk Guarantees for ECSC Loans

The Directorate of Credit and Investments
Batiment Wagner
Kirchberg
Luxembourg L1907
Tel: 010 352 430 16190

Coal Areas
British Coal Enterprise Ltd
Eastwood Hall
Eastwood
Notts NG16 3EB
Tel: 0773-531313

Steel Areas
BS Industry
Canterbury House
2–6 Sydenham Road
Croydon CR9 2LJ
Tel: 081-686 2311

Rail Areas
British Rail Engineering
St. Peter's House
Gower Street
Derby DE1 1AH
Tel: 0332 383850

Contact points for other grants

Urban Areas
Department of the Environment
Inner Cities Division
Room P2/119
2 Marsham Street
London SW1P 3EB
Tel: 071-276 4488

City Grants
Department of the Environment
Inner Cities Division
Room P2/127
2 Marsham Street
London SW1P 3EB
Tel: 071-276 4507/4506

Derelict Land Grant
Department of the Environment
Inner Cities Division
Room P2/109
2 Marsham Street
London SW1P 3EB
Tel: 071-276 4466

Rural Development Commission
11 Cowley Street
London SW1P 3NA
Tel: 071-222 9134

Enterprise Zones
A list of Central Government and local contact points is available from:

Department of the Environment
Inner Cities Division
Room P2/110
2 Marsham Street
London SW1P 3EB
Tel: 071-276 4488

Appendix 2

Sources of help and advice

Housing/House Prices
Information on home search services; housing; house prices.

Association of Relocation Agents
105 Hanover Street
Edinburgh EH2 1DJ
Telephone: 031-220 2505

National Mobility Office
35 Great Smith Street
London SW1P 3BJ
Telephone: 071-222 0356

Halifax Building Society
Head Office
Trinity Road
Halifax
W. Yorks
HX1 2RG
Telephone: 0422 365777

Nationwide Anglia Building
Society
New Oxford House
High Holborn
London WC1V 6PW
Telephone: 071-242 8822

National Federation of Housing
Associations
175 Grays Inn Road
London WC1X 8UP
Telephone: 071-278 6571

Woolwich Equitable Building
Society
Equitable House
London SE18 6AB
Telephone: 071-854 2400

Equity Sharing/Equity Mortgage
Kleinwort Benson Ltd
20 Fenchurch Street
London EC3P 3DB
Telephone: 071-623 8000

Marriott, Harrison, Bloom and
Norris
34 Bedford Row
London WC1R 4JH
Telephone: 071-405 7954

Management consultants
Location decision advice, site selection, project management.

Clark Whitehall Consultants Ltd
25 New Street Square
London EC4A 3LN
Telephone: 071-353 1577

Debenham, Tewson & Chinnocks
44 Brook Street
London W1A 4NA
Telephone: 071-408 1161

DPM Services Ltd
19 Short's Gardens
Covent Garden
London WC2H 9AT
Telephone: 071-379 0270

Ernst & Young
Rolls House
7 Rolls Buildings
Fetter Lane
London EC4A 1NH
Telephone: 071-831 7130

P A Management Consultants
68 Knightsbridge
London SW1X 7JL
Telephone: 071-589 7050

Peat Marwick McLintock
Management Consultants
1 Puddle Dock
Blackfriars
London EC4V 3PD
Telephone: 071-236 8000

P-E Group
Park House
Wick Road
Egham
Surrey
TW20 0HW
Telephone: 0784 434411

Price Waterhouse Management
Consultants
Thames Court
1 Victoria Street
Windsor
Berks
SL4 1HB
Telephone: 0753 868202

Property Spectrum Ltd
Nelson House
19 West Street
Carshalton
Surrey
SM5 2PT
Telephone: 081-669 6927

Pugh Carmichael Consultants
250 Kings Road
London SW3 5UE
Telephone: 071-351 7655

Information provision/communications/counselling
Information packs, presentations, communication material, exhibitions, tours, employee and spouse counselling.

Dow Sheppard Relocation Services
63 High Street
Shrivenham
Swindon
Wilts
SN6 8AW
Telephone: 0793 782214

National Startpoint
Prospect House
Brunswick Terrace
Stafford
ST16 1BD
Telephone: 0785 43235

PMA Ltd
Trend House
Dallow Road
Luton
Bedfordshire
LU1 1BY
Telephone: 0582 400184

Trotman & Co Ltd
12-14 Hill Rise
Richmond
Surrey
TW10 6UA
Telephone: 081-940 5668

Government departments
Publications, circulars, advice on: regional aid; tax.

Department of Trade and Industry
Kingsgate House
66-74 Victoria Street
London SW1E 6SW
Telephone: 071-215 7877

Inland Revenue
Public Enquiry Room
West Wing
Somerset House
London WC2R 1LB
Telephone: 071-438 6420

Labour market
Information on labour availability, labour market structure.

Ecotec Research & Consulting Ltd
Priory House
18 Steelhouse Lane
Birmingham
B4 6BJ
Telephone: 021-236 9991

Relocation management companies
Relocation management companies offer a range of services including: guaranteed home sale; price disparity analysis; group move consulting and management; policy consultation; communication programmes; employee counselling; area information packs; home search; removals management.

ARC Relocation Ltd
ARC House
11/13 The Broadway
Newbury
Berks RG13 1AS
Telephone: 0635 30622

Hambro Countrywide Relocation
22 Commercial Way
Woking
Surrey
GU21 1HB
Telephone: 0483 770071

Black Horse Relocation Services
59-60 Thames Street
Windsor
Berks
SL4 1TX
Telephone: 0753 850581

Hamptons Relocation
Cherry Orchard North
Kembrey Park
Swindon
Wiltshire
SN2 6BL
Telephone: 0793 619555

IRC Worldwide Ltd
Premier House
10 Greycoat Place
London SW1P 1SB
Telephone: 071-222 8866

Merrill Lynch Relocation Management International Ltd
136 New Bond Street
London W1Y 3FA
Telephone: 071-629 8222

Morton Fraser Relocation Ltd
15 & 19 York Place
Edinburgh
EH1 3EL
Telephone: 031 557 4903

National & Provincial Relocation
Provincial House
Bradford
West Yorkshire
BD1 1NL
Telephone: 0274 733444

Nationwide Anglia Relocation
Chineham Court
Great Binfields Road
Chineham
Basingstoke
Hants RG24 0YJ
Telephone: 0256 842395

PHH Homequity Ltd
PHH Centre
Windmill Hill
Whitehill Way
Swindon
Wilts SN5 9YT
Telephone: 0793 887000

Simmons Relocation Services Ltd
5 Campden Street
Kensington
London W8 7EP
Telephone: 071-727 4602

Tavistock Relocation Management Ltd
Tavistock House
34 Bromham Road
Bedford
MK40 2QD
Telephone: 0234 213571

Education consultants/research
Identification of suitable schools/education facilities, counselling, education research

Dean Associates
51 High Street
Emsworth
Hampshire
PO10 7AN
Telephone: 0243 378022

Educational Relocation Associates
13 Feltham Road
Ashford
Middlesex
TW15 1DQ
Telephone: 0784 248353

University of Sheffield
MRC/ESRC Social and Applied Psychology Unit
Sheffield
N. Yorks
S10 2TN
Telephone: 0742 756600

Employee Relocation Councils
Conferences, seminars, research reports, magazines, policy libraries, enquiry service, directories, lobbying service.

CBI Employee Relocation Council
Centre Point
103 New Oxford Street
London WC1A 1DU
Telephone: 071-379 7400

Employee Relocation Council
1720 N Street, N.W.
Washington
DC 20036
USA
Telephone: 0101 202 857 0857

Canadian Employee Relocation
Council
20 Eglinton Avenue West
Box 2033
Suite 1202
Toronto
Ontario
M4R 1K8
Canada
Telephone: 0101 416 489 2555

Research/publications
Pay, benefits, allowances and company practice published in surveys and studies.

Incomes Data Services Ltd
193 St. John Street
London
EC1V 4LS
Telephone: 071-250 3434

Industrial Relations Services Ltd
18-20 Highbury Place
London
N5 1QP
Telephone: 071-354 5858

Institute of Manpower Studies
The Mantell Building
University of Sussex
Falmer
Brighton
BN1 9RF
Telephone: 0273 686751

The Reward Group
Reward House
Diamond Way
Stone Industrial Estate
Stone
Staffordshire
ST15 0SD
Telephone: 0785 813566

Libraries

These libraries are available for use by members.

Institute of Personnel Management
IPM House
Camp Road
Wimbledon
London SW19 4UW
Telephone: 081-946 9100

Industrial Society
3 Carlton House Terrace
London SW1Y 5DG
Telephone: 071-839 4300

British Institute of Management
Management House
Cottingham Road
Corby
Northants
NN17 1TT
Telephone: 0536 204222

Briefing/cultural awareness training

Briefing, cultural awareness and language training, cost of living data.

The Centre for International
Briefing
Farnham Castle
Farnham
Surrey
GU9 0AG
Telephone: 0252 721194

Organization Resources
Counselors Inc
Suite 22
78 Buckingham Gate
London SW1E 6PE
Telephone: 071-222 9321

Employment Conditions Abroad
Ltd
Anchor House
15 Britten House
London SW3 3TY
Telephone: 071-351 7151

Bibliography

Books and reports

ALAN JONES & ASSOCIATES. *Relocation policy survey report.* Monmouth, Alan Jones & Associates, January 1989.

COYLE, WENDY. *On the move – minimising the stress and maximising the benefit of relocation.* Sydney, Australia, Hampden Press, 1988.

INCOMES DATA SERVICES LTD. *Relocation – study No 399.* London, Incomes Data Services Ltd, 1987.

INCOMES DATA SERVICES LTD. *Group relocation – study No 448.* London, Incomes Data Services Ltd, 1989.

INLAND REVENUE. *Extra-statutory concessions.* UK, HMSO, 1988.

INSTITUTE OF MANPOWER STUDIES. *Relocating managers and professional staff – IMS report No 139.* Brighton, Institute of Manpower Studies, 1987.

MERRILL LYNCH RELOCATION MANAGEMENT INTERNATIONAL LTD. *Fourth annual study of employee relocation policies among UK companies.* London, Merrill Lynch Relocation Management International, 1987.

MERRILL LYNCH RELOCATION MANAGEMENT INTERNATIONAL LTD. *Fifth annual study of employee relocation policies among UK companies.* London, Merrill Lynch Relocation Management International, 1988.

MUNTON, TONY. *An investigation into managerial job relocation: stress and mobility.* Sheffield, Sheffield University, 1988.

PRICE WATERHOUSE *and* CBI EMPLOYEE RELOCATION COUNCIL. *Moving experiences.* London, Price Waterhouse and CBI Employee Relocation Council, 1989.

SHORTLAND, SUE. *Managing relocation.* Basingstoke, Macmillan Press, 1987.

Journal articles

BEAUMONT, STELLA. 'Why today's workers are on the move'. *Personnel Management.* Vol. 21, No. 4, April 1989. pp. 42–46.

CRAIG, ROSALIND. 'The role of crisis counselling in UK relocation'. *Relocation News.* No. 2, Autumn 1986. p. 5.

FOSTER, JOANNA. 'Mobility and equal opportunities'. *Relocation News.* No. 7, July 1988. pp. 5–7.

GRAHAM, S. *and* CAIRNS, A. 'Company relocation – identifying personnel concerns'. *Relocation News.* No. 6, Spring 1988. pp. 13–17.

GREENBURY, LINDA. 'Relocating the working wife'. *Relocation News.* No. 5, January 1988. pp. 3–5.

GUEST, DAVID. 'Relocation and stress'. *Relocation News.* No. 6, Spring 1988. pp. 19–21.

HOWSON, JOHN. 'Education and domestic relocation'. *Relocation News.* No. 11, July 1989. pp. 17–18.

INDUSTRIAL RELATIONS LEGAL INFORMATION BULLETIN. 'Relocation and employment law'. *Industrial Relations Legal Information Bulletin.* No. 316, November 1986. pp. 2–9.

INDUSTRIAL RELATIONS REVIEW AND REPORT. 'Moving with a purpose – head office relocations'. *Industrial Relations Review and Report.* No. 413, March 1988. pp. 2–8.

INDUSTRIAL RELATIONS REVIEW AND REPORT. 'Relocation survey 1: background and trends'. *Industrial Relations Review and Report.* No. 432, January 1989. pp. 6–11.

INDUSTRIAL RELATIONS REVIEW AND REPORT. 'Relocation survey 2: high cost moves'. *Industrial Relations Review and Report.* No. 433, February 1989. pp. 6–10.

INDUSTRIAL RELATIONS REVIEW AND REPORT. 'Relocation survey 3: controlling costs, administration and eligibility'. *Industrial Relations Review and Report.* No. 436, March 1989. pp. 6–11.

INDUSTRIAL RELATIONS REVIEW AND REPORT. 'Relocation survey 4: scheme basics, bridging loans and disturbance allowances'. *Industrial Relations Review and Report.* No. 437, April 1989. pp. 6–14.

JENKINS, SUSAN. 'Instructing solicitors on house moves: questions and answers'. *Relocation News.* No. 9, January 1989. pp. 7–9.

LANE CLARK, PHILIP. 'The contribution of assessibility studies to relocation'. *Relocation News.* No. 8, October 1988. pp. 7–8.

MITCHELL, STUART. 'Guaranteed price: practical implications'. *Relocation News.* No. 4, Autumn 1987. pp. 7–10.

MUNTON, TONY. 'Education concerns'. *Relocation News.* No. 10, April 1989. pp. 3–5.

PAYNTER, MICHAEL. 'Equity sharing'. *Relocation News.* No. 7, July 1988. p. 8.

PENZER, NIGEL. 'Legal aspects of relocation transactions'. *Relocation News.* No 3, Spring 1987. pp. 19–20.

RELOCATION NEWS. 'Short distance moves'. *Relocation News.* No. 3, Spring 1987. pp 13–17.

RELOCATION NEWS. 'Home sale: principles and practice'. *Relocation News.* No. 4, Autumn 1987. pp. 3–7.

RELOCATION NEWS. 'Helping to overcome the house price divide'. *Relocation News.* No. 5, January 1988. pp. 7–8.

RELOCATION NEWS. 'Home search: domestic moves'. *Relocation News.* No. 6, Spring 1988. pp. 3–5.

RELOCATION NEWS. 'Relocation and the law'. *Relocation News*. No. 6, Spring 1988. pp. 7–8.

SCHOFIELD, PHILIP. 'Employee communications – company moves within Britain'. *Relocation News*. No. 9, January 1989. pp. 14–15.

SHORTLAND, SUE. 'Managing relocation – the Royal Bank of Scotland'. *Industrial Relations Review and Report*. No. 425, October 1989.

SHORTLAND, SUE. 'Managing relocation – Rhône-Poulenc'. *Industrial Relations Review and Report*. No. 426, October 1989. pp. 8–10.

STEWART, CLAIRE. 'The importance of briefing in international relocation'. *Relocation News*. No. 3, Spring 1987. pp. 2–5.

Index

195